W9-BWT-278

HEALTHCARE MADE EASY

ANSWERS TO ALL OF YOUR HEALTHCARE QUESTIONS UNDER THE AFFORDABLE

MICHELLE KATZ, MSN, LPN

adamsmedia

Avon, Massachusetts

Published by
Adams Media, a division of F+W Media, Inc.
57 Littlefield Street, Avon, MA 02322. U.S.A.
www.adamsmedia.com

ISBN 10: 1-4405-8019-7
ISBN 13: 978-1-4405-8019-2
eISBN 10: 1-4405-8020-0
eISBN 13: 978-1-4405-8020-8

Printed in the United States of America.

10   9   8   7   6   5   4   3   2   1

Library of Congress Cataloging-in-Publication Data

Katz, Michelle.
    Healthcare made easy / Michelle Katz, MSN, LPN.
        pages cm
    Includes index.
    ISBN 978-1-4405-8109-2 (pb) -- ISBN 1-4405-8019-7 (pb) -- ISBN 978-1-4405-8020-8
(ebook) -- ISBN 1-4405-8020-0 (ebook)
    1. Health insurance--Government policy--United States. 2. Medical policy--United States.
3. Medical care--United States. 4. United States. Patient Protection and Affordable Care
Act. I. Title.
    RA412.2.K37 2014
    368.38'200973--dc23
                                    2014028824

Author photo by Nadia Tyson (*http://nadiatyson.com*).
Author's hairstyle by Vanessa Dena from Salon Viva (*www.salonviva.co*).

This book is available at quantity discounts for bulk purchases.
For information, please call 1-800-289-0963.

ACKNOWLEDGMENTS

Through my clinical and administrative experiences in the healthcare industry, as well as my own struggles with medical-care costs, I have gained a greater understanding on how to become a smarter healthcare consumer. I am thankful to everyone who has supported me through this learning process. Thanks to all who have shared their knowledge and expertise with me. A special thanks goes out to Christopher Condeluci of Venable, LLP; Robert Graboyes and Richard Williams of the Mercatus Center at George Mason University; Bob Fairbairn of the David M. Gilston Insurance Agency; the Public Relations Department at the Kaiser Foundation; Tasha Bradley and Lorraine Ryan of the Centers for Medicare & Medicaid Services; Kaelon Hollon of PhRMA.org; John Daly of BlogTalkRadio.com; Lindsey Mask, founder of Ladies America; and Bonnie McDaniel of the Women Are Talking initiative.

I would like to thank my ABC family, especially my *Real Money* team including Eric Noll, Paula Faris, Rebecca Jarvis, and the families that allowed me to tell their stories on air. A special thanks goes to Diane Sawyer who followed my work for all these years, gave me encouragement, and believed in what I was doing. She really made those broadcasts possible.

I'd be remiss not to thank the team at Adams Media for helping to make this book possible—Brendan O'Neill, Peter Archer, and Jennifer Lawler. Also a big thanks goes to Kristen Tomaiolo, my indispensable intern and research assistant. I am deeply indebted to my literary agent, Kevin Moran, for his fortitude, advice, and counsel. He really helped to make this book a reality.

Finally, and most important, my deepest thanks to my dear friends the Lowrance family, who supported and inspired me to fulfill a dream and encouraged me through the toughest of obstacles. And to my

Facebook, Twitter, and Instagram communities that kept me on my toes with some great questions that will be answered in this book. All your "likes" keep me going.

—Michelle Katz

CONTENTS

PART 4:

CONTROLLING YOUR HEALTHCARE COSTS 153

INTRODUCTION

Whether you agree with it or not, the Affordable Care Act, otherwise known as Obamacare, is here to stay, and it will affect all of us in one way or another. Sections of the law may change slightly in the next few years, keeping those in Congress busy and the rest of us on our toes, but the basic structures of this law will, in all likelihood, remain the same.

The Affordable Care Act is a comprehensive healthcare insurance reform act that provides certain benefits to, and requires certain actions from, all Americans. For example, under the terms of the act, in general everyone must be covered under a health insurance plan, by enrolling in a plan offered at your place of employment, or through a group policy offered by another type of organization, or by purchasing an individual policy. A health insurance marketplace (which we'll sometimes just call the Marketplace) has been set up to help you do this. If you fail to obtain health insurance coverage, you face a penalty.

People who have difficulty paying for their health insurance may qualify for a federal subsidy that will help them, or they may qualify for assistance under expanded Medicaid programs. (Medicaid programs are state-run programs designed to help low-income residents obtain needed healthcare.)

One of the main purposes of the ACA is to reduce the overall number of Americans who don't have health insurance. In May 2013, this number of uninsured under the age of sixty-five (and therefore not eligible for Medicare, the federal program that provides health insurance for the elderly and some younger people) was estimated to be about 57 million Americans, a number many experts believe would have continued to rise without the ACA.

Two of the main benefits of the ACA are the most popular:

1. Health insurance companies can no longer refuse to issue a policy to you based on a preexisting medical condition.
2. Young adults, up to age twenty-six, can continue to be covered under a parent's policy.

There are other benefits as well, and of course there are some drawbacks. For example, as you may have learned, if you have an insurance plan that does not meet the ACA's minimum requirements for health insurance, it will be canceled and you'll have to enroll in a new plan. (There are some exceptions to this, as we'll see.)

The ACA is intended to improve the efficiency of the overall healthcare system, to reduce overall healthcare costs, and to improve health outcomes for Americans, including those who have traditionally had less access to healthcare. How successful the ACA is in accomplishing these goals remains to be seen.

The purpose of this book is to help guide you through the complexities of the law so that you have a clearer understanding of how the Affordable Care Act works, how it affects you, and the steps you'll need to take in order to follow its rules and to experience some of its benefits.

The book is divided into four sections. The first section covers what the Affordable Care Act is and does. The second guides you in selecting a healthcare plan. The third shows you how to use your benefits. The fourth and final section offers suggestions for how to control your healthcare costs. The conclusion provides additional resources for further questions. In the appendix, you'll also find some information on choosing a doctor.

Most of the material is set up in a question-and-answer format so that you can quickly find answers to your most important questions about the ACA.

Let's get started!

PART 1

HOW THE AFFORDABLE CARE ACT AFFECTS YOU

You may feel as if understanding the ACA requires you to keep an attorney on speed dial just to answer your questions—and you probably have a lot of questions! It probably seems as if every time you answer one question, another one pops up.

However, while the ACA can seem like a big, overwhelming mass of confusing terminology and complicated requirements, you'll be able to understand the whole thing if you just take it a step at a time. That's what this book is designed to help you do. It *is* possible to boil down all of the jargon and government-issued statements into plain English.

In Part 1, I've created a series of questions and answers to help you understand what the ACA is, how it affects you, and what steps you need to take in order to meet its requirements. This section will help you understand the basic parts of the law that directly affect individual consumers (like you!). It will define the most common terms you'll encounter in dealing with the law, describe the building blocks of the law so that you understand their purpose and how they affect you, and explain some of the systems that have been put in place in order for the law to be carried out, such as healthcare exchanges (the Marketplace).

After reading this section you might just start scratching your head and saying, "My goodness, I didn't know it was that easy." At least, I hope so.

BASIC TERMINOLOGY

What exactly is the healthcare exchange (also called the insurance exchange, or the health insurance marketplace)?

You've probably been hearing a lot about this because there were a number of glitches when it first rolled out. Set up under the Affordable Care Act, it's a new way to find healthcare coverage. It went into effect with a lot of fanfare on October 1, 2013 for individuals and small business owners who have lost their coverage or who do not already have it.

Basically, you go to a central website and compare the various health insurance options available in your state, as provided by various private companies. You can sign up for your health insurance through the website. You can also determine if you are eligible for a financial subsidy or if you qualify for a state Medicaid program. If you have trouble understanding the options, you can call a navigator or meet with one in person.

What's the difference between a state-run exchange and the federal exchange?

You'll use the exchange that is relevant to your state, and the exchanges vary from state to state. You can find out what kind of state exchange/

marketplace you are living in by going to *www.statereforum.org/where -states-stand-on-exchanges*.

If you're living in a state that is implementing a State-Based Marketplace (SBM), that means the state government is responsible for all plan functions: quality healthcare plans; premium fees; oversight/monitoring/eligibility/enrollment; outreach/education; and consumer complaints.

If you live in a state that's implementing a Partnership Marketplace, these responsibilities are taken over by the federal government, although the state government has responsibility for plan management and/or consumer assistance.

Finally, if your state has a federally facilitated Marketplace, that means all these functions are the responsibility of the federal government.

Some of the exchanges work better than others, but it's fair to say that in any case you'll need a little patience to use any of them effectively.

What are essential health benefits?

The Affordable Care Act specifies that all private insurance companies must cover at least ten categories of benefits; these are called essential health benefits (EHB). Each state decides the specifics of coverage, so exactly what form your coverage in each of these categories takes depends on where you live and which insurance company you pick. You can check the guidelines for your state at *www.cms.gov/ CCIIO/Resources/Data-Resources/ehb.html*.

If you belong to a large group plan (as opposed to small group or individual plan insurance) or a plan that's grandfathered into the system, these plans aren't required to carry essential health benefits.

Any plans that do carry EHB must remove annual and lifetime dollar amounts for those services.

One thing more: As the ACA finds its footing, it's possible that more essential health benefits might be added, which could increase insurance premiums. However, that's in the future.

Can you describe what some of these Essential Health Benefits are in greater detail?

Yes! Here are some of the EHBs:

1. **Ambulatory patient services.** If you visit your doctor's office for a visit and aren't admitted to a hospital, this is the kind of care you're receiving ("ambulatory" means you can walk out of the office under your own power). It also refers to home health and hospice care, though in these cases coverage may be limited to forty-five days. However, if you go to a neighborhood clinic, your doctor's office, or a same-day surgery center, those services are covered.

2. **Emergency services.** Of course, no one likes to think about going to the ER for any reason, but it's comforting to know that under the ACA, you cannot be penalized for going out-of-network or not having prior authorization to do so. If you or your family find yourself in circumstances in which a condition, if not immediately treated, will lead to serious disability or death, the ACA protects you from higher copayments and coinsurance if you wind up in an out-of-network ER.

3. **Hospitalization.** This is among the most potentially expensive healthcare you can receive. It includes room and board in the hospital, as well as physician and nursing care, tests, drugs, and a lot of other miscellaneous charges. It also covers surgeries, transplants, and care you receive in a skilled nursing facility (such as a nursing home). Note that some plans limit skilled nursing facility coverage to forty-five days. It would be nice if the insurance companies paid your entire bill, but they don't. Depending on your plan, you may still be responsible for 20 percent or more of the bill—more if you haven't reached your out-of-pocket limit. Since some hospitals charge as much as $3,000 per day for room and board (and that doesn't include the medical stuff), hospitalization can take a big bite out of your wallet.

4. **Maternity and newborn care.** Amid the excitement of a new baby's arrival, most people probably don't want to consider their budgets, but you should. This EHB refers to care that women receive during pregnancy, birth, and post-delivery, as well as care for the baby itself. ACA says that prenatal care must be provided without extra cost, but some other services will probably require a charge. For instance, insurance plans under ACA must provide breastfeeding support, counseling, and equipment for the duration of breastfeeding, but the specifics of what's covered may be different from plan to plan. Your doctor will determine what kind of breastfeeding plan you need, and most insurance plans will follow the doctor's recommendations. In some cases, you may need preauthorization. Under ACA, most insurance plans will cover the cost of a breast pump (either rental or yours to keep). Ask if the plan provides guidance as to whether the pump can be

manual or electric, how long the coverage lasts, and where you can get the pump.

Other services in this category of EHB that may be offered by various plans include:

- Testing for sexually transmitted diseases
- Rh blood typing and antibody testing
- Folic acid supplements, which help protect your baby from certain birth defects
- A wide range of prenatal tests, including anemia screening, UTI screening, and screening and help to quit tobacco use
- Testing for gestational diabetes
- Birth control after the birth of your baby

Be sure to check and make sure your plan covers these items before your doctor prescribes them or administers the tests.

5. **Mental health and substance use disorder services, including behavioral health treatment.** One in four adults, or about 61 million people in the United States, experiences some form of mental illness in a given year. About 13.7 million have serious illnesses such as schizophrenia, major depression, or bipolar disorder. Even greater numbers suffer from drug abuse. The ACA mandates coverage of inpatient and outpatient services for such disorders, though some plans may limit this to twenty days per year. These services must provide evaluation, diagnosis, and treatment. This is another instance in which exactly what is covered and how the insurance is provided will vary from state to state. For more information, go to *www.mentalhealth.gov.*

6. **Rehabilitative and habilitative services and devices.** If you have sustained an injury, you'll probably need some sort of physical therapy to regain the functionality you've

lost. In general, insurance plans must cover at least thirty visits a year for occupational, physical, chiropractic, speech, or cardiac therapy and pulmonary rehabilitation. As well, the plans must cover devices such as canes, wheelchairs, and crutches that will be needed while the therapy is in progress.

- *Habilitative services* are services that allow you to acquire a functional skill you should have but don't because of sickness or injury (for instance, speech therapy for an autistic child). Things are a bit less clear with long-term disease treatment such as multiple sclerosis, and you'll need to check with your plan to find out the extent of its coverage.
- *Rehabilitative services* are services that allow you to get back a skill you lost because of illness or an injury. For instance, if you've suffered a stroke, you'll need physical or occupational therapy to regain motor functions.

7. **Laboratory services.** To come up with an accurate diagnosis of your ailment and the appropriate treatment, your doctor conducts all sorts of tests. The ACA mandates insurance plans to cover laboratory tests; however, it's up to you to find out the scope of this coverage—what tests are covered, which laboratories, and what physicians can prescribe laboratory work. If your doctor recommends a lab that isn't outlined in your insurance plan, ask the plan provider if there's a replacement or if they anticipate accepting that lab in the future.

8. **Preventive and wellness services and chronic disease management.** Not all illnesses and conditions go away after a single treatment or even a series of treatments. Some can last a very long time—even a lifetime. This EBH includes anything from annual physicals to

immunizations and cancer screenings designed to prevent or detect certain medical conditions, as well as assist in the care and management for chronic conditions such as asthma and diabetes. For more detail on this, go to *www.healthcare.gov/what-are-my-preventive-care-benefits/*. Be sure to call your provider ahead of time to find out the exact details of coverage because although things such as breast cancer screenings, Pap smears, and prostate exams may be given free of charge, you may still be billed for diagnostic tests that doctors order when you have symptoms of disease. Costs for these tests can range from $20 for a lab test to 30 percent of the cost of a magnetic resonance imaging scan (MRI), which can mean hundreds to thousands of dollars if you are not careful.

9. **Pediatric services.** If you're wondering how your children will fare under the Affordable Care Act, the answer is, pretty well. Children under age nineteen are entitled to get their teeth cleaned twice a year, as well as receive x-rays, fillings, and medically necessary orthodontia. Children under age nineteen are also entitled to an eye exam and one pair of glasses or set of contact lenses a year. In addition, insurance plans must cover well-child visits and recommended vaccines and immunizations. Remember that you will have to have a plan that covers your family if you want your child to have coverage. (A spouse can also be covered under a family plan.)

10. **Prescriptions.** Who doesn't know the irritation of standing in line at the pharmacy to get your prescription filled, wondering how much this is going to cost you? The ACA can't do away with all that uncertainty, but it does mandate that Marketplace plans must cover at least one drug in every category and class in the U.S. *Pharmacopeia*, the official

publication that lists approved medications. In addition, pharmaceutical costs are counted toward out-of-pocket caps on medical expenses, as opposed to separate caps as some companies used to do.

What qualifies as essential minimum coverage?

As you've probably heard, the ACA requires you to have health insurance. If you don't have it, you must pay a penalty. Minimum essential coverage refers to the least amount of coverage you need in order to avoid paying that penalty.

To be clear, it's not enough to have only coverage for a specific kind of health-related issue. If you only have vision care, dental care, or coverage for a particular disease or condition (such as a cancer policy), that's not going to cut it. These policies can be a useful supplemental insurance that can help you pay some bills not covered under your regular health insurance policy but they do not qualify as minimum essential coverage under the ACA.

Following is a list of plans that *do* qualify as minimum essential coverage under the ACA:

- A qualified health plan offered by the health insurance marketplace
- Medicare Part A
- Medicare Advantage plans

- Most Medicaid coverage
- Children's Health Insurance Program (CHIP) coverage
- Certain types of veterans health coverage administered by the Veterans Administration
- Most types of TRICARE coverage under Chapter 55 of Title 10 of the United States Code
- Coverage provided to Peace Corps volunteers
- Coverage under the Nonappropriated Fund Health Benefit Program
- Refugee Medical Assistance supported by the Administration for Children and Families
- Self-funded health coverage offered to students by universities for plan or policy years that begin on or before December 31, 2014 (for later plan or policy years, sponsors of these programs may apply to HHS to be recognized as minimum essential coverage)
- State high-risk pools for plan or policy years that begin on or before December 31, 2014 (for later plan or policy years, sponsors of these programs may apply to HHS to be recognized as minimum essential coverage)
- Other coverage recognized by the Secretary of HHS as minimum essential coverage
- Employer-sponsored coverage, including self-insured plans, COBRA coverage, and retiree coverage

If your existing plan isn't one of these, don't panic. Call your health insurance company and ask them if their plan qualifies as minimum essential coverage.

Are there any exemptions from the requirement to obtain minimum essential coverage?

You may not have to pay a penalty for being uninsured if you can prove you qualify for one of these nine exemptions (for more information and to find the forms you need to apply for an exemption, go to *www.healthcare.gov/exemptions/*):

1. **Religious conscience.** Do you belong to a religious sect, as defined by the Social Security Administration, that is recognized as conscientiously opposed to accepting any insurance benefits?
2. **Healthcare sharing ministry.** Are you a member of a recognized healthcare sharing ministry?
3. **Indian (Native American) tribes.** Do you belong to an Indian tribe recognized by the federal government? Are you eligible for services through an Indian care provider?
4. **Income below the income tax return filing requirement.** Is your income below the minimum threshold for filing a tax return? Here is a tool to help determine if you are required to file a federal tax return: *www.irs.gov/uac/Do-I-Need-to-File-a-Tax-Return%3F*.
5. **Short coverage gap.** Have you gone without coverage for less than three consecutive months during the year? (This one is to help people who are between jobs.)
6. **Hardship.** Have you suffered a hardship that makes you unable to obtain coverage? You can download a document outlining the different kinds of hardships at the IRS website: *www.irs.gov*.

7. **Affordability.** Can you not afford coverage? This is a pretty common issue. The ACA says that if the minimum amount you must pay for the premiums is more than 8 percent of your household income, you're eligible for this exemption.
8. **Not lawfully present.** Are you not a U.S. citizen, a U.S. national, or an alien lawfully present in the United States?
9. **Incarceration.** Are you in a penal institution or correctional facility after the disposition of charges against you?

So what happens if you don't qualify for any of these exemptions and you decide you're still not going to buy health insurance? Well, as I said earlier, you have to pay a penalty. And who collects that penalty? The IRS, and no one wants to mess with them.

How will the IRS decide if you have health insurance? You may have noticed when filing your taxes in the past year, there was a box asking if you have health insurance. You might have overlooked it . . . or maybe you chose to overlook it. This is where the IRS gets their information. However, and it's a big however, the IRS can only collect the penalty if you are getting money back on your tax return. If not, you might get a sternly worded letter from the IRS, but that's it.

Keep in mind, though, that if you choose to pay the penalty, whether the IRS collects it or not, at the end of the day you still don't have health insurance, and if you become ill and need extensive medical care, you're going to get socked with a hefty bill from the doctor's office. And *they* won't stop at sending you a sternly worded letter.

What is the new "80/20 rule" exactly?

The "80/20 rule" is the nickname for the Medical Loss Ratio (MLR) rule.

One of the goals of the ACA is to rein in costs not associated with caring for patients' health and to make healthcare costs more even nationwide, rather than varying widely from state to state.

The 80/20 rule says that insurance companies have to disclose how much they spend on actual healthcare and how much they spend on administrative costs. Essentially, insurance companies can no longer hike up premiums to pad their own profits and boost bonuses for their executives. The company must spend at least 80 percent of your premium dollar on your healthcare or improving that care and only 20 percent on things related to the company's administration. If the company spends more than that 20 percent on administrative issues, it has to rebate the overage to you.

Keep in mind that the first report was filed in 2012 for the 2011 year, so do not expect a rebate check for years prior to 2011, unless you have an extremely generous insurance company. However, if you are entitled to a rebate, the insurance company will notify you by August 1 of each year (for overages from the previous year).

The rebate won't necessarily come as a check in the mail. It could be:

- a lump sum reimbursement to the credit/debit card you used to pay the premium
- a reduction in your future premiums
- if you are receiving your plan through your employer, a payment by your company to you in one of the previous ways. The company can also apply the rebate in a way that benefits the employees.

There's one very big exception to the 80/20 rule: It doesn't apply to employers who have fewer than 1,000 enrollees in a particular state.

Nor does it apply to those employers who operate a self-insured plan. This is a plan in which a group (in this case, the employer) rather than an insurance company assumes financial responsibility for the medical expenses. Since it's difficult to tell if you have one of these plans, the best thing is to ask your employer what type of plan you're on.

- If you're not on a self-insured plan, find out if you'll be receiving a rebate (that is, if the insurer has spent more than 20 percent of your premium on costs not directly related to your medical needs) and if so, what form the rebate will take.
- If you are on a self-insured plan, sit down and go over the benefits as well as the provider network.

Can I keep my existing plan? If not, why not?

Of all the questions about the Affordable Care Act, this is one of the most frequently asked. It's become a major political hot button in the ongoing debate about the act.

The answer is a qualified "yes." If you purchased your plan on or before March 23, 2010, it will be grandfathered—that is, it will be allowed under the ACA and you'll be able to keep it (see the section called "Grandfathered Insurance Plans" in this part for more information on grandfathered plans).

However, as of 2015 if your plan isn't grandfathered and doesn't meet the ACA's requirements, you'll have to get a new plan. However, the government can't just take your plan away from you. Your provider must notify you and provide you with other options.

The key to all this is finding the plan that works best for you (and your family, if applicable). Although you may not like the options you're offered, keep in mind that healthcare is changing fast and new plans are becoming available every month.

If your plan doesn't qualify under the ACA as acceptable coverage, it's possible that's because:

- It doesn't offer free preventive services and wellness visits
- It denies treatment or coverage for preexisting conditions
- It doesn't offer the ten essential health benefits required by the ACA with no annual or lifetime dollar limits
- It permits cancellation for providing bad information if that information is the result of a clear mistake on the part of the enrollee, and it doesn't offer a right of appeal
- It allows discrimination based on gender or health
- It doesn't offer a ban on all lifetime dollar limits

The basic point here is that if you can't keep your old plan, there's a very good reason for it: The plan isn't providing the kind of insurance you need. For that reason, you need to switch to a new plan. However, don't feel you're getting locked into something. If you choose a plan and find it's not for you, you can change plans at the next open enrollment period.

You may also qualify to change plans outside of the open enrollment period if you have a major life event such as marriage or the birth of a child.

PAYING FOR HEALTH INSURANCE

Do I qualify for subsidies? What should I do if I do not?

You may feel that purchasing health insurance is prohibitively expensive based on your income. The federal government does provide some subsidies to help lower-income individuals afford coverage. Whether you qualify for a subsidy will depend on many factors. The main three are:

- Your household income
- The number of your dependents
- In what part of the country you are located

Take the following steps to see if you qualify for subsidies:

1. Estimate your income. When you fill out the application, you'll be using your *modified adjusted gross income (modified AGI)*. Your *adjusted gross income (AGI)* is the total amount of money you made last year minus certain items (e.g., any expenses from a business you own, health savings account deductions, certain moving expenses, etc.). You can find your AGI on line 20 of your income tax Form 1040 (line 4 on Form 1040EZ). Your *modified AGI* may include some items that were excluded from your AGI. For more information on how to calculate your modified AGI, the IRS website provides this article: *www.irs.com/articles/what-modified*

-adjusted-gross-income. Or, check with a financial advisor about how to make this calculation.

2. List your household dependents and their income (if they have any).

3. Now that you've got an income number, go to *www.health care.gov* and shop around for a plan you like. Depending on which plan you select and what information you put in, the site will tell you whether or not you qualify for subsidies.

Unfortunately, some states are not participating in the Medicaid expansion program (which is intended to provide more healthcare services to a broader range of lower-income individuals), so subsidies in these states may be a little scarcer. To find out if your state is expanding Medicaid coverage, go to *www.healthcare.gov/what-if-my-state-is-not -expanding-medicaid/*.

If your state is *not* expanding Medicaid, and you have a limited income but don't qualify for Medicaid under your state's current rules, you may be able to get low-cost healthcare at a Community Health Center near you. Here's the link to click to find out more about this: *www.healthcare.gov/where-can-i-get-free-or-low-cost-care/*. Here is a helpful subsidy calculator to see if you qualify: *www.kff.org /interactive/subsidy-calculator/*.

My income is too high for subsidies. Now what?

I know it can be frustrating if you seem to be just getting by but are deemed to be making too much money to qualify for a subsidy. Here are some suggestions:

- Go through the insurance company, not the Marketplace. Try calling the insurance company directly. Unfortunately, this may be more difficult in some states than others, but you may be able to get straight answers from someone who is extremely knowledgeable about their company's products.
- Solicit help from an insurance agent or broker. Just be sure the broker is representing a number of insurance companies instead of only one. Keep in mind that some brokers/agents may not be completely transparent, especially if one insurance company is paying them more commission than another. Be sure to ask how many plans are in their portfolio. Do they seem to be pushing you to choose one plan over another? Remember, this is your decision, not theirs, and you have to live with it until the next open enrollment period.
- Investigate a health insurance seller online. Don't feel pressured to buy anything in one day, but use this research as a reference guide to compare plans.

Once you've made a list of plans, compare them to what you're finding on the health insurance marketplace at *www.healthcare.gov/how-do-i-apply-for-marketplace-coverage/*.

Be sure to check and double check your options. Keep in mind that even if you are unable to get lower costs on monthly premiums based on your income, you might be able to save on some out-of-pocket costs by selecting a higher deductible, as well as qualify for a premium tax credit. This credit is for anyone purchasing health insurance through the health insurance marketplace. For more information, go to *www.irs.gov/uac/The-Premium-Tax-Credit*.

How do the fair health insurance premiums affect me?

Before the passage of the Affordable Care Act, insurance companies could adjust your premium rates based on things like your health status, medical history, gender, and the industry in which you worked. All that changed with the ACA. Today insurance premiums can *only* vary based on your age, whether you use tobacco products, your family size, and where you live. How does this work in practice?

Here are the basics:

1. The older you are, the more premiums may cost you. If you're older, you might pay more. For example, children up to twenty years of age will pay the least amount out of all age groups, and there will be no variation in rates between different ages within this range (these ranges are called bands). If you are an adult between twenty-one and sixty-three, your premium rate will go up slightly every year until you are sixty-four years of age. After that, you'll continue to pay the same amount. One feature of the new system is that the ratio between the age groups has been reduced to 3:1. In other words, a company can charge someone in the sixty-four-and-over band up to three times the amount they're charging someone in the twenty-and-under band, but no more. This is a change from the previous 5:1 ratio. States can also use a narrower ratio with the approval of the Centers for Medicare and Medicaid Services (CMS) and a person's age for rating purposes if their age changes at the time of the policy's effective/renewal date.

2. If you smoke, expect to pay a higher premium. This doesn't apply to tobacco used for religious and ceremonial purposes,

but if you enjoy a pipe, cigarettes, or cigars, keep in mind that's going to cost you in healthcare premiums. This applies if you're eighteen or older and have used tobacco products four or more times a week within the past six months. Under the ACA, your insurance company can charge you up to 50 percent more for your premiums if you use tobacco recreationally.

3. If you have a bigger family, your premium will be higher. Your household size is determined by how many people you're claiming as dependents on your tax return. There's a cap of three on the number of children who can be covered under an individual family policy; if you have more than three children, you'll have to apply for a group policy.

Also consider that because premium prices vary from state to state and from city to city, you may have to move to get a better rate. According to *Kaiser Health News*, if you have decided to buy the Silver plan in the Marketplace you may be paying more for your health insurance premiums if you live in Alaska, the Colorado ski resort towns, Connecticut (Fairfield specifically), southern Georgia, southeast Mississippi, rural Nevada, far western Wisconsin, Wyoming, and Vermont.

For a summary of ACA costs state by state, go to *www.legalconsumer .com/obamacare/welcome.php*.

How can I determine my household size so that I can better estimate how much my premiums will cost?

To figure out your household size, consider the following:

- If you live alone and have no dependents, or you live with roommates and have no dependents, your household size is one.
- If you are married and have two children who are dependents, you are considered to have a household size of four.
- If your spouse or one of your children has health insurance elsewhere—for example from work, or on a government program such as Medicaid—your household size will still be four since that person is still considered a dependent on your taxes.
- If your mother, father, brothers, sisters, aunts, uncles, or other family members live with you and are dependents they are also counted in the household size. So, if your grandmother lives with you and your spouse and your two children, your household size is five, even if your grandmother has Medicare, Medicare Advantage, or some other health coverage. She will not be covered under the Marketplace health insurance because she has health insurance through one of these programs, but she is still included in the household size.
- If one of your family members, such as a grandparent, lives with you, but she or he is *not* a dependent, meaning his or her income is not included in your family income, he or she is *not* counted in your household size.
- If you and your spouse are separated and have been living apart for the past six months, the person who is caring for a dependent child can claim a special filing status that will *not* include the other person's income. Your household size will be two (you and the child).

What are the financial penalties for not maintaining health insurance coverage?

As mentioned earlier in this section, if you don't qualify for an exemption from the ACA rules about health insurance and you still decide you don't want to purchase insurance, you're going to pay a penalty. This is also the case if you *do* have a plan but it doesn't meet the ACA's standards for minimum essential coverage (although, as mentioned previously, there are some exceptions to this). The penalty may not seem like very much the first year, but every year you put off getting insurance or moving to a new plan that fits within the system, the amount you pay will increase. Here's how it works:

1. In 2014, the penalty is 1 percent of your annual household income above the tax return filing threshold of $10,150 (but no more than the national average annual premium for a Bronze plan, the least expensive plan within the system), **or** $95 per adult and $47.50 for each child under eighteen years old ($285 in total for a household), whichever is higher.
2. In 2015, the penalty goes up, to either 2 percent of your annual household income, or $325 per adult and $162.50 per child under eighteen (whichever is higher). The maximum penalty takes a big jump to $975.
3. In 2016 and beyond, the penalty is 2.5 percent of your annual household income, or $695 per adult and $347.50 per child. The maximum household penalty is $2,085.

The penalty will continue to rise in subsequent years.

As you can see, the purpose of the penalty is to persuade you to get coverage and to get it sooner rather than later. It's important to remember that if you pay the penalty, that doesn't mean you have insurance. If you get sick and have to go to the hospital, you'll still pay a lot of money. For more on these penalties, go to *www.healthcare.gov /what-if-i-dont-have-health-coverage/*.

What's my penalty if I only have health insurance for part of the year?

If you are uninsured for only part of the year, the penalty is prorated so you won't wind up paying the full amount. For example, if you're only insured half the year, you'll pay a penalty that's half the normal amount. However, for gaps in coverage of less than three months you won't be subject to a penalty. Beyond 2016, the penalties and fees involved in the ACA will be subject to cost-of-living increases.

When is it better to pay the penalty?

Generally speaking, it's better to get the insurance, since the last thing you want to do is play Russian roulette with your healthcare and wind up owing hospitals and doctors thousands (or hundreds of thousands) of dollars.

The only time you should even think of paying the penalty is if you're generally healthy and have a solid network of providers with whom you've pre-negotiated rates and caps on costs.

In that case, add up the amount you would be paying for your premiums, copayments, coinsurance, and consider the out-of-pocket maximum that may come your way this year. If—and it's a very big *if*—the amount is more than the penalty, you can pay the penalty and save yourself some money. Two things to keep in mind, though:

1. The penalty costs go up each year, so you need to continually reevaluate your decision not to purchase insurance.
2. Catastrophic healthcare incidents are, well, catastrophic—that is, they're unforeseeable. Even your most careful planning can go awry.

More information about not having health insurance can be found at *www.healthcare.gov/what-if-someone-doesnt-have-health-coverage-in-2014/*. In addition, you can use the handy "penalty calculator" found here: *www.calculator.taxpolicycenter.org.*

If you decide not to get insurance, I'd strongly advise you to start investing more money in your 401(k) account. If you use the distribution to pay for unreimbursed medication expenses that are more than 10 percent of your adjusted gross income, you won't have to pay an early withdrawal penalty to the bank. Keep in mind that medical expenses are generally high and can drain your savings very quickly.

Do I have to buy health insurance in 2014 if I cannot afford it?

It's possible that your financial circumstances currently preclude buying health insurance. Perhaps you're out of work or have incurred some other massive debt that needs to be paid off. You may decide to have only catastrophic coverage through the Marketplace—that is, you may be able to buy insurance that gets around some of the ACA's rules and is therefore cheaper. You may be exempt from paying the penalty if you can prove one of the following hardships, as defined by the Department of Health and Human Services (HHS):

- You recently experienced domestic violence.
- A close family member recently died.
- You experienced a natural (fire, flood, etc.) or human-caused disaster that caused substantial damage to your property.
- You are/were homeless.
- You're facing eviction or foreclosure, or have been evicted in the past six months.
- You received a shut-off notice from a utility company based on nonpayment because you could not afford the bill (not because you forgot).
- You filed for bankruptcy in the past six months.
- You had medical expenses you couldn't pay in the past twenty-four months.
- Your expenses went up because you are caring for an ill, disabled, or aging family member.
- You don't have to pay a penalty for a child if you expect to claim him/her as a tax dependent who has been denied coverage in Medicaid and CHIP, and another person is required by court order to give medical support to this child.
- You were ineligible for Medicaid because your state didn't expand eligibility for Medicaid under the ACA.
- Your individual insurance plan was canceled and you believe other Marketplace plans are unaffordable (described next).

If you don't qualify for any of these hardship circumstances but the plans mandated by the ACA still seem unaffordable to you, you may qualify for an "unaffordable" exemption. That means that the premiums of the plan you want to buy exceed 8 percent of your annual income. For example, if you have no dependents and an annual household income of $60,000, your healthcare premiums should not exceed $4,800 for that year, or it would be considered unaffordable.

What if I have a gap in coverage of less than three months?

It's possible that a change in your employment situation will mean that you go for a short period without coverage. If this is less than three months, don't worry about a penalty; everyone is allowed one three-month gap per year without having to pay a penalty for not carrying health insurance.

If you've decided to strike out on your own and start a business, instead of risking an extended gap in coverage (and paying a penalty), you can purchase an individual (or family) insurance policy on the exchange, or you can look around for an organization that offers group plans such as the local Chamber of Commerce, college alumni associations, some religious associations, and other groups. Naturally, before signing up you should review the policy to make sure you can afford the premiums and that it meets the ACA's minimum essential standards (not to mention your basic health needs). Do due diligence with these plans as you would with any other.

GRANDFATHERED INSURANCE PLANS

What is a grandfathered health insurance plan?

If you purchased an individual health insurance policy on or before March 23, 2010, you should be able to keep it, even if it doesn't meet all of the requirements mandated by the ACA. These plans are "grandfathered" into the system set up by the ACA.

However—and this is where a lot of the controversy comes in—some of these grandfathered plans lost their grandfathered status because they made significant changes that reduced benefits or increased the costs to consumers. Other plans decided not to offer a grandfathered plan, which is why many people lost their plans in the past. If that happened to you or is in the process of happening, the insurance provider must provide notice ninety days before the plan ends, as well as offer you other available coverage options.

The best source of information as to whether your plan is grandfathered is your health insurance provider. If the plan considers itself grandfathered, the materials you received should say that somewhere. The provider should also advise you to contact the U.S. Department of Labor or the Department of Health and Human Services about questions.

Despite the cutoff date of March 23, 2010, new employees and family members may be added to grandfathered group plans after that date.

If you have a grandfathered plan through work, you are not excluded from joining an individual plan under the Marketplace. You should weigh all your options for you and your family, since it could be cheaper due to subsidies and extra benefits you might be missing out on. For more on this, look at *www.healthcare.gov/what-if-i-have-a-grandfathered-health-plan/*.

What does a grandfathered plan have to cover?

Grandfathered plans can differ significantly from essential coverage mandated by the ACA in the following areas:

1. *Essential benefits coverage.* A grandfathered health plan doesn't have to provide certain preventive services to you at no cost. These include mammograms, contraceptive coverage, at least one annual checkup and blood test, and other preventive or screening services. For more information, go to *www.healthcare.gov/how-does-the-health-care-law-protect-me/#part=8*.

2. *Preexisting conditions.* Grandfathered plans that you purchase as an individual policy can deny you coverage or increase your premiums for preexisting conditions you may have. For more information go to *www.healthcare.gov/how-does-the-health-care-law-protect-me/#part=3*.

3. *Providers.* Whereas Marketplace plans must allow providers to participate as long as they operate within the scope of their license, this doesn't apply to grandfathered plans. Even if the provider is willing to accept a health insurer's terms and conditions for participation in provision of services, a grandfathered plan isn't obligated to let the provider

do so. For more information, go to: *www.healthcare.gov/how -does-the-health-care-law-protect-me/#part=6*.

4. *Emergency services.* Under the terms of the ACA, insurance plans must cover emergency services even if you didn't get preauthorization (which, when you think about it, is really good, since you might be unconscious in the immediate aftermath of the emergency). Your insurance plan also can't impose any administrative requirement or limitation on benefits for out-of-network emergency services that is more restrictive than the requirements or limitations that apply to in-network emergency services. In addition, a plan can't impose a copayment or coinsurance amount for out-of-network emergency services that is greater than the amount that would apply if the services had been provided in-network. However, if your plan is grandfathered, it doesn't have to meet these requirements.

5. *Premium rates.* The ACA sets limits on what your insurance provider can charge you for premiums, depending on your age, tobacco usage, and so on. Remember that under the ACA, you can only be charged a maximum 3:1 difference based on age (compared to the youngest group). In addition, if your provider wants to raise your rates more than 10 percent, they have to publicly justify such a rate increase. However, none of this applies to grandfathered plans.

6. *Appeals process.* Under the ACA, if you're denied services, there's an appeals process you can go through to dispute your provider's action. Grandfathered plans are not required to provide this process. For more information, go to: *www.healthcare.gov/how-does-the-health-care-law-protect -me/#part=11*.

7. *Clinical trials.* In the past, many insurance plans have denied coverage for participants in clinical trials. Marketplace

plans under the ACA are required to provide health insurance to enrollees in such trials. However, grandfathered plans are not required to do so.

8. *Annual and lifetime limits.* Under the ACA, insurance companies aren't allowed to set annual or lifetime coverage expenses limits for essential health benefits. This doesn't apply to grandfathered plans. For more information go to: *www.healthcare.gov/how-does-the-health-care-law-protect-me /#part=9.*

9. *Frivolous cancellations.* If you make a mistake on your policy—say you write down the wrong number in the wrong box or misremember your spouse's date of birth—the ACA does not allow your provider to cancel your policy. The only grounds for policy cancellation are if you don't pay your premiums or if you intentionally lie on your application (and if either of these is the case, the provider must notify you within thirty days that your policy will be canceled). However, if you have a grandfathered plan, it may be under no such obligation.

10. *Coverage for young adults.* One aspect of the Affordable Care Act that's received a great deal of attention is that it mandates that young adult dependents must be covered until they are twenty-six years old. This doesn't necessarily apply under a grandfathered plan.

11. *Summary of benefits.* All Marketplace plans under the ACA must contain a simple summary of benefits with a glossary of terms so you can compare plans and decide on the one best for you and your family. You can also request a copy of this information in your native language. However, grandfathered plans aren't obligated to do this.

Is it possible for my plan to lose its grandfathered status?

Yes. Your plan can be deprived of its grandfathered status if it has done any of the following things since March 23, 2010:

1. *Made a significant cut or reduction in benefits.* For instance, if it has eliminated all or most of the benefits used to diagnose and treat a particular condition, this will cause the plan to lose its grandfathered status. For example, if your insurance announces that it's no longer going to cover counseling for a mental disorder, this will trigger a loss of grandfathered status.

2. *Increased coinsurance charges.* If, in March 2010, your plan had a 10 percent coinsurance rate (meaning you were responsible for 10 percent of charges) and at a later date changed that rate to 20 percent, meaning your financial responsibility for your medical coverage went up from 10 percent to 20 percent, your plan would lose its grandfathered status.

3. *Had a rise in fixed costs sharing.* Fixed costs include everything from deductibles to out-of-pocket limits. The rule is that these costs can't go up in one jump by more than the cost of medical inflation (currently set at 9.5 percent) plus 15 percent. In practical terms, this means that if one year your plan had a deductible of $2,500 and an out-of-pocket maximum of $5,000, the next year it could increase the deductible to $2,700 and the out-of-pocket limit to $5,600. Any more and the plan would lose its grandfathered status.

4. *Raised copayment charges.* Plans are allowed to keep their grandfathered status and still raise copayments by

medical inflation (remember, we said that's 9.5 percent) plus 15 percent; or, increase copayments by $5, whichever of these two things is greater. If your plan raises your copayments by any more than that, it will lose its grandfathered status.

5. *Added or narrowed an annual limit.* For example, a plan that previously had no limit on MRIs could not impose a $5,000 per year maximum on MRIs without losing its grandfathered status.

It's extremely important to be aware of these conditions, because if your plan loses its grandfathered status, you may have to get another plan.

Can my plan's grandfathered status be lost if my employer is providing the plan?

Yes. There are three circumstances in which an employer-provided plan that's grandfathered can lose that status:

1. When your employer's contributions are lowered by 5 percent for any group of covered persons. For example, let's say in March 2010 your employer contributed 90 percent of the cost of employee-only coverage and 70 percent of the cost of family coverage. After that date, the company you work for kept the employee-only contribution the same but it reduced its contribution for family coverage to 60 percent. Under these circumstances the plan will lose grandfathered status.

2. If your employer reclassifies employees so that they are eligible for a different plan (even if it's a grandfathered plan).
3. If the employer fails to continuously maintain at least one covered individual in the plan.

I figured out that I have a grandfathered plan, but it's made some changes. Now what?

Don't panic. Even if your grandfathered plan made changes after March 2010, this doesn't automatically mean you'll have to find a new plan. If the plan didn't violate any of the conditions discussed in the previous questions, it still retains its grandfathered status, and you can keep it.

However, it's possible that your insurance provider may decide to discontinue your plan, forcing you to get a new one. If this has happened, you should be given reasonable notice and options for finding new coverage.

I haven't heard anything from my insurance provider. Does that mean my plan is grandfathered?

If your insurance plan is about to lose its grandfathered status, you should receive a notice from your provider. If you haven't received a notice, your plan may have fallen into one of these three categories:

1. It's unchanged and has been grandfathered into the Affordable Care Act.
2. Your plan met the requirements of the ACA, so there's no need to grandfather it.
3. You have Medicare, Medicaid, TRICARE, or another form of public healthcare, so the issue doesn't come up.

Make sure that your provider has your correct address; letters have been known to go astray.

THE APPEALS PROCESS

If you've ever been upset with a decision your insurance company has made and have tried to appeal their decision, you know how difficult and frustrating this process can be. How many of you ever appealed a decision, got a denial on your first attempt, and went back for a second or even third attempt? Not many, I'm guessing. That's why the appeals process has a special section written into ACA with guidelines that must be followed. It's meant to make this process easier for you.

Under the Affordable Care Act, how does the appeals process work?

Generally, there are two ways to appeal your health plan's decision under the ACA: the internal appeal and the external review.

1. In the internal appeal, your insurance company will conduct a "full and fair review" of its decision.
2. In the external review process, you have the right to take your appeal to an independent third party for review, which means that the insurance company will no longer get the final say over whether to pay a claim.

In most cases, an external review can only be done after an internal review has been completed; however, if the insurer has not fulfilled its obligations in the internal appeals process, you may immediately file an external appeal. During these review processes, your insurer cannot reduce or stop coverage for ongoing treatment. If you would like more information on filing an eligibility appeal you can call 1-800-318-2596 or TTY: 1-855-889-4325.

What's involved in the internal appeals process?

You or your healthcare provider will file a claim with your insurance company, requesting reimbursement for services. If the company decides to deny the claim, they must notify you in writing with an explanation for their decision within the following time frames:

- Fifteen days if you're seeking prior authorization for a treatment
- Thirty days for medical services you've already received
- Seventy-two hours for urgent-care cases

Once you receive notice of a denial of claim, you have 180 days to file an internal appeal; if your situation is urgent, you can jump to the external appeal immediately. After the insurance company conducts the review of your appeal, they must provide their decision to you in writing. At this point, assuming they're still denying your claim, you have the option to file an external appeal; the company must provide you with directions about how to do this.

What if my care is urgent and I need an expedited decision?

Many people have an urgent situation at least once in their life. If that's true of your situation, you can request an external review, even if you have not completed all of the insurance plan's internal appeals processes. You can even file an internal and external appeal at the same time, if necessary. If the standard appeal process will seriously jeopardize your life or ability to regain maximum function, you can file an expedited appeal, which must be completed within four business days after your request is received. The final decision can be delivered verbally and must followed by a written notice within forty-eight hours.

What does an external review process entail?

If you've chosen an experimental treatment or your insurer says you filed false or incomplete information when applying for benefits and the company denies your claim, you're more likely to get an external review.

Your explanation of benefits (EOB) or the written denial of your internal appeal will give you the contact information for the organization that will handle your external review, should you choose to file one. In most cases, you must first file a written request for an external review within sixty days (although some may allow for a little more time) of the date your insurer sent you a final decision. Your insurer is required by law to accept the external reviewer's decision.

A state list maintained by the Department of Health and Human Services (HHS)'s Center for Consumer Information and Insurance Oversight can be found at *www.cms.gov/cciio/resources/files/external_appeals.html*.

Unfortunately, some states do not have an external review process that meets the minimum consumer protection standards. In states that do not have the review process in place, the HHS will oversee an external review process. If you live in such a state, call 1-888-866-6205 to request an external review request form. In addition, I suggest faxing an external review request to 1-888-866-6190. Fill out as much of the form as you can and have your doctor fill out what you could not, with supplemental information that may help your case. Send the forms to MAXIMUS Federal Services, 3750 Monroe Avenue, Suite 705, Pittsford, NY, 14534. You can also submit a request via e-mail to ferp@maximus.com or you can file a request electronically through *www.externalappeal.com*. If you need more help filling out your external review, your state's Consumer Assistance Program (CAP) or department of insurance may be able to help you.

MANAGING YOUR HEALTHCARE PLAN

Under the ACA, can my coverage be canceled? If so, under what circumstances?

Yes, your coverage can be canceled. However, this isn't anything new; prior to the implementation of the Affordable Care Act, health insurance plans were canceled all the time. The difference now has to do with the acceptable reasons for the cancellation.

As indicated previously, your insurance plan may be canceled for any of the following reasons:

- The plan did not meet the standards outlined in the ACA rules
- The plan was previously grandfathered into the system, but lost its grandfathered status because it made unauthorized changes (see the section on "Grandfathered Insurance Plans" in this part)
- Your provider decided to discontinue the plan that covers you and your family
- You committed fraud in applying for coverage or claims

In cases where your action(s) caused cancellation of coverage, you have a right of appeal, as outlined in the earlier section called "The Appeals Process."

So my insurance provider can just stop offering my policy?

Under the Health Insurance Portability and Accountability Act (HIPAA), individual policies are generally renewed at the end of the twelve-month contract. As long as your insurer has met the following requirements, it can stop offering your policy:

- A written notice must be sent to each covered individual within ninety days. A word of caution here: Make sure your insurance company has your updated contact information. If you've moved recently or are lucky enough to have multiple residences, you may find that a notice was sent to the wrong residence. If written notice was sent within ninety days and you were not there to receive it, the company can still cancel your policy.
- Covered individuals (you and your family members) must be offered the option to buy any other individual policy offered by the insurer to individuals in that market.
- All covered individuals must be treated the same.

If your insurer chose to discontinue all health insurance in your state's individual market, it can discontinue an individual policy without offering you the chance to buy a new policy. If this is the case, your insurer is prohibited from offering coverage in that state's individual market again for five years (which can put a real damper on their business) and it must notify all policyholders and the state of its decision at least 180 days before stopping coverage. You should notify your state's department of insurance if you feel that your insurer is not following these requirements. Keep in mind that additional requirements may apply, depending on what state you are located in.

The only way to make the best and most informed decisions for you and your family is to become an educated consumer. Shop around at least three months before open enrollment so you know your options, and make sure your health insurance provider has your correct and most updated information so they can alert you of policy changes throughout the year.

Can I shop on the exchange (the Marketplace) even if my employer offers healthcare?

Of course you can. In fact, I encourage it. You might even be able to enlighten your employer as to what other options are out there that offer more choices at a lesser cost. However, if you decide to leave your work-based plan and purchase coverage on the Marketplace, you may not qualify for some of the benefits you might be receiving on your employer-based plan, or vice versa.

For example, you may only be eligible for government subsidies on your insurance if your employer's coverage for an individual is considered unaffordable under the law or if your employer's insurance coverage/cost sharing is considered inadequate (for example, picking up less than 60 percent of the cost of covered benefits). In addition, if you decide to switch to an individual plan, be sure your providers accept the new Marketplace plan. If you have benefits such as dental and vision care, you might want to reconsider sticking with your work-based plan because these are not part of the essential health benefits that must be offered by plans for sale on the Marketplace.

What are private exchanges?

These are healthcare exchanges created by private companies. They normally operate both online and through human advocacy and are designed to help you find the right plan for you and your family. If your plan hasn't been canceled and has been grandfathered in, or it may be noncompliant but still exists, you're under a private exchange. This means you're exempt from the ACA-imposed penalty for not having insurance (since you're on a plan).

However, if you leave that plan for any reason, chances are you won't be able to get back on it and you'll have to enter a Marketplace plan under the ACA. Private plans can offer other medical benefits (dental, vision, etc.) not offered by the public exchanges. However, the private exchanges don't offer government subsidies, as do the public ones.

What are the four types of plans I can choose from through the public Marketplace exchanges?

The plans are named for metals: Bronze, Silver, Gold, and Platinum, in ascending order of benefits and expense:

1. **Bronze plan:** This is the least expensive, covering about 60 percent of your medical expenses (plus or minus 2 percent). You'll have the lowest monthly premiums of the four plans, but you'll also have the highest out-of-pocket costs.
2. **Silver plan:** This plan will cover about 70 percent of your medical expenses. The remaining 30 percent will be out-of-pocket

costs to you. The premiums are a bit higher than the Bronze plan, but the direct cost to you in terms of expenses is lower.

3. **Gold plan:** The Gold healthcare plan pays about 80 percent of your medical costs. It has the second-highest premiums of the plans. Keep in mind that the precise costs will vary from company to company and state to state.

4. **Platinum plan:** This is the most expensive plan in terms of premiums. It will cover 90 percent of healthcare costs, and you'll pay the other 10 percent. Again, premiums for different companies will vary.

What's the open enrollment period?

This is when you can enroll in an insurance plan, using either public or private healthcare exchanges. However, if you just began a new job and your employer is part of a group market, such as the Small Business Health Options Plan (SHOP), you are allowed to enroll year-round. That's true as long as the employer meets the contribution or minimum participation requirements for the group market. Your company's HR department will be able to tell you if they're part of this market and what your enrollment dates are.

Are there any other exceptions to the open enrollment dates?

Yes. The following situations can create a sixty-day enrollment period for the special and limited open enrollment periods in the individual markets (this may be limited to thirty days in the group markets).

- If you've experienced marriage, birth, adoption, or placement for adoption
- If you need new coverage as a result of a permanent move
- If you lose minimum essential coverage through your existing plan
- If you make mistakes during your regular enrollment that result in a loss of coverage
- If your provider incurs a major violation of the insurance contract
- If you've become newly eligible or newly ineligible for advance payments of the premium tax credit or have experienced a change in eligibility for cost-sharing reductions

What's covered for me and my child under the new Child Health Insurance Program (CHIP) laws?

Under the Affordable Care Act, every state must provide comprehensive coverage for children including routine checkups, immunizations, doctor visits, prescriptions, dental and vision care, inpatient and outpatient hospital care, laboratory and radiology (x-ray) services, and emergency services. To find out more details on your state-specific program, go to *www.insurekidsnow.gov/state/index.html.*

How does the ACA affect out-of-pocket maximums, deductibles, coinsurance, and copays?

The ACA requires that health plans consider deductibles, copays, and coinsurance all part of the out-of-pocket maximums, which is the most you will pay during a policy year before your insurance plan starts to pay 100 percent of essential covered benefits.

Let's break this down a little further:

- Copays are the flat fees you pay to a provider for a specific service. For instance, you may have a copay of $50 every time you visit your doctor's office. Depending on your doctor and your relationship, this copay can be waived.
- A deductible is the amount of money you must pay your provider for services before your insurance company starts paying. For instance, if you have a deductible of $1,500, you'll pay for the first $1,500 of your medical expenses, after which a portion of them will be paid by your insurance company.

The maximum out-of-pocket cost limit for any individual Marketplace plan for 2014 can be no more than $6,350 for an individual plan and $12,700 for a family plan. However, this number will increase every year according to inflation rates.

In the past, most policies did not have a limit on the deductibles, and copays were not included in the out-of-pocket maximum. Under the ACA, the only exceptions to the out-of-pocket limits are some grandfathered plans and some business plans that have until 2015 to comply.

The out-of-pocket limit required by the ACA does not have to count premiums, your increased costs for going out-of-network, or spending for nonessential health benefits.

So if I hit my out-of-pocket maximum, does that mean everything else is covered?

No. Unfortunately, you'll still have to pay your health insurance premiums, any items not covered by your health plan (for instance, cosmetic surgery), items your insurer deems to be not medically necessary, and any out-of-network expenses that are your responsibility.

It's important to know what providers are in the network and which ones aren't, as well as the type of plan you have. If your health insurance plan does not accept your preferred provider (or your healthcare provider does not accept your insurance), your medical expenses will not be covered, no matter what your maximum out-of-pocket is.

What are the drug prescription benefits under the ACA?

In the past, you may have found that prescriptions were not covered under your health insurance plan, or were considered to have a separate out-of-pocket maximum as well as a separate deductible. That's now changed.

Under the Affordable Care Act, not only does every health plan have to offer prescription drug coverage, but the costs of any medications your doctor prescribes are also put toward your out-of-pocket maximum, as well as your deductible. Thus prescription coverage isn't separated out from medical coverage.

In addition, each state sets its own list of covered medicines that every plan within that state must offer. This is called the formulary and specifies the bare minimum your health insurance must include. Your health insurance plan may actually offer more medicines. Most of these formularies have tiers that define their cost. Typically the higher the tier, the higher the cost:

- Tier 1: Generic medicines (cheapest).
- Tier 2: Preferred brand-name medicines.
- Tier 3: Nonpreferred brand-name medicines.
- Tier 4: Specialty medicines, usually the most expensive. For example, chemotherapy drugs will probably fall into the fourth tier.

The practical implication of this is that before you purchase a health insurance plan, be sure it includes the medications you need, as well as medications you may prefer when you get sick. If the brand-name medication isn't available through your plan, determine whether you can use the generic version.

For example, if your plan doesn't offer the antibiotic Trimox, which your doctor usually prescribes for your child every time he or she gets an ear infection, find out if its generic, amoxicillin, is offered on your plan. You also need to check with the doctor to find out if it's okay to use the generic drug in place of the brand-name medicine.

It is also important to check on the maximum dosage your health insurance allows your doctor to prescribe before you need to get a refill (not having to refill your prescription as often can save you money, as will be described in Part 4).

Medications can be added or removed from the formularies at any time, but the insurance plan needs to notify its beneficiaries of this in writing. The most common changes are generic drugs replacing brand-name drugs, especially as brand-name drugs go off-patent, but sometimes one generic drug will replace another.

If you cannot find the prescription of your choice on a health plan's drug list in the Marketplace, all is not lost. You can request that your plan cover it or give you access to it, and you can enlist your doctor to explain the medical need for this. However, if the plan covers the generic version rather than the brand-name drug, it's unlikely the insurance company will extend its coverage to the brand-name medicine. If your request is denied, you have the right to appeal your health plan's decision. The appeals process is explained in the section earlier in this part called "The Appeals Process."

What is a multi-state plan?

This is a health insurance plan, administered by the U.S. Office of Personnel Management (OPM) and covered within the exchanges/marketplaces, that allows families and small businesses that are spread out over more than one state to select a health plan from the same health insurance issuer. This type of coverage is expected to be available in all states by 2017 and will expand into the Small Business Health Options Program (SHOP) exchange markets over time. (Note that at the time of this writing, the legislation on this is still being ironed out.)

Under the law, insurers participating in the multi-state program must offer at least two plans through each exchange—one at the

Silver level of coverage and one at the Gold level. (These terms refer to the average percentage of medical costs a plan is required to cover. Silver plans on average will cover 70 percent of an enrollee's medical costs, and Gold plans will cover about 80 percent.) For more information, go to *www.opm.gov/healthcare-insurance/multi-state-plan -program.*

THE ACA AND SELF-EMPLOYMENT

How does the ACA affect self-employed people?

More than 9 million people in the United States are self-employed. If you're one of them, you probably want to stay self-employed and get health benefits under the ACA. If you work for yourself, in order to avoid penalties or fees under the ACA, you must have either minimum essential coverage or qualify for an exemption.

If you are self-employed, it may be difficult to find coverage that's affordable. If this is the case, you may find that you qualify for an individual tax credit as well as some subsidies on a sliding scale, based on your income. In addition, you may be in luck if you live in a state that has decided to expand Medicaid eligibility. This expansion includes adults ages nineteen to sixty-four with incomes up to 133 percent of the Federal Poverty Level (which is about $15,000 per year for an individual and $31,000 per year for a family of four), but not all states have expanded eligibility.

What's the Small Business Health Operations Program (SHOP)?

Yes, I know. The acronym really should be SBHOP. But it isn't. Here's what the deal is:

SHOP is an exchange for businesses with fifty full-time employees or fewer that allows you to offer healthcare coverage to your workers. Keep in mind that as a business of this size, you're not required to offer any coverage. However, if you want to do so you can choose among the following options:

- Allow your employees to choose any plan offered through SHOP at any level of coverage
- Select specific levels of coverage from which your employees can choose a plan
- Select specific plans from which your employees can choose
- Select a single plan and offer it to all your employees

If you have fewer than twenty-five employees and you get insurance through SHOP, you may be eligible for tax credits. You can investigate this more by going to *www.healthcare.gov/what-is-the-shop-marketplace/*.

You can start this coverage any time. If you enroll on the fifteenth of the month, coverage will start at the beginning of the subsequent month.

Rules vary from state to state; in a lot of states as many as 70 percent of your full-time employees will have to enroll in the insurance you offer. Also note that in 2016 the definition of a small business will change to one that employs up to 100 full-time workers.

A few other points:

- Eligible employers must have an office within the service area of the SHOP.
- Small employers must offer SHOP coverage to all full-time employees.
- The Department of Health and Human Services (HHS) has a call center hotline that specifically serves small businesses with fifty or fewer employees interested in purchasing coverage through the SHOP Marketplace. The phone number is 1-800-706-7893, Monday through Friday, 9 A.M. to 5 P.M. EST.

As a small business owner, am I eligible for any healthcare-related tax credits?

Yes, indeed! Earlier in this section, I mentioned that if you employ twenty-five or fewer full-time workers and purchase health coverage through SHOP, you're eligible for a tax credit. In addition, you may qualify for this credit if:

- If the total annual wages you pay out are less than $50,000
- If you contribute 50 percent or more toward your employees' self-only health insurance premiums

Use the Small Business Healthcare Credit Estimator at *www .taxpayeradvocate.irs.gov/calculator/SBHCTC.htm* to help you find out whether you're eligible for the credit and how much you might receive.

What notices do I have to give to my employees?

If your business has at least one employee and does an annual business volume of at least $500,000, you were required to have given notification to your employees about the new health insurance Marketplace by October 1, 2013. This includes:

- Informing employees that they may be eligible for a premium tax credit if they purchase coverage through the Marketplace.
- Advising workers that if they purchase a plan through the Marketplace, they may lose the employer contribution (if any) to any health benefits plan you as the employer offer them.

If you choose not to offer a health plan, you must give your employees the form you'll find at *www.dol.gov/ebsa/FLSAwithoutplans .doc*. If you offer your workers a health plan, distribute the form you can download at *www.dol.gov/ebsa/pdf/FLSAwithplans.pdf*.

As a small business owner, am I eligible for rebates under the 80/20 rule?

In the section on "Basic Terminology" earlier in this part, we talked about the 80/20 rule. Remember the idea is that an insurance provider is mandated to spend at least 80 percent of your premium on things that directly impact your healthcare and only 20 percent (or less) on things like administrative costs, upkeep, etc. If the provider doesn't do this, it's obligated to give rebates to its policyholders.

The answer to the question is yes, as a small employer holding a group policy you are entitled to a rebate. You then have to decide how to treat the rebate: Will you reinvest it in the plan or will you return it to the employees?

What other changes has the ACA made that are important to small businesses?

Quite a few. Here are some of the major ones:

- If your company offers healthcare flexible spending accounts (FSAs) through a cafeteria plan, beginning January 2013 an employee can contribute up to a maximum cap of $2,500 to his or her FSA. This doesn't, however, affect the employer contribution.
- There has been an increase in Medicare withholding from wages, which you, as the employer, are required to withhold. For employees with incomes of more than $200,000 as single filers and $250,000 for married filers, the ACA has increased the employee part of Medicare Part A Hospital Insurance withholdings from 1.45 percent to 2.35 percent.
- As of January 1, 2014, anyone who's eligible for employer-provided healthcare coverage won't have to wait more than ninety days for the coverage to start.
- Beginning in 2014 and running through 2016, a program called the Transitional Reinsurance Program reimburses insurers for high claims costs. As an employer providing insurance to

your employees, you'll help pay for this program through fees (estimated in the first year by Health and Human Services at around $63 per year per person insured). You can take some comfort from the fact that the fees are tax deductible.

What does the insurance I'm offering my workers have to cover?

There are ten services ("essential health benefits") your plan must cover: ambulatory patient services; emergency services; hospitalization; maternity and newborn care; mental health and substance use disorder services, including behavioral health treatment; prescription drugs; rehabilitative and habilitative services and devices; pediatric services; laboratory services; and preventive and wellness services and chronic disease management.

This will vary somewhat from state to state, but these are the basic features of what your plan must offer your workers.

Beginning in January 2016 the HHS will review these benefits, so they may change in future.

Anything else I should know about my employer insurance plan?

Yes. It has to offer the four levels of coverage discussed in the section on "Managing Your Healthcare Plan": Bronze, Silver, Gold, and Platinum. Remember that:

- Bronze: insurance pays 60 percent; employee pays 40 percent
- Silver: insurance pays 70 percent; employee pays 30 percent
- Gold: insurance pays 80 percent; employee pays 20 percent
- Platinum: insurance pays 90 percent; employee pays 10 percent

Also, small group plans can't have an annual deductible of more than $2,000 for single coverage and $4,000 for family coverage (this will be adjusted every year for inflation). Furthermore, insurance premiums can only be adjusted by age and tobacco use, with the same guidelines regarding ratios that we outlined in the section on "Basic Terminology."

Finally, all small employers in the small group market are treated as part of a single risk pool. Health risks inside *and* outside the SHOP exchange are pooled together.

DETERMINING THE SIZE OF YOUR COMPANY

For purposes of health insurance under the Affordable Care Act, what determines the size of my company?

There are a couple of factors that will help you determine this:

- How many full-time employees you employ. The small business group market is currently defined as having fifty or fewer full-time or full-time equivalent (FTE) workers. However, in 2016, the small business cap will increase to 100 full-time employees.

- Whether your company offers minimal essential coverage to full-time employees and their dependents.
- If one or more of your full-time employees qualifies for government subsidies toward the purchase of health insurance on the individual exchange. (Note that a worker qualifies for a subsidy if his or her required contribution to their premiums is higher than 9.5 percent of taxable income).

What's a full-time employee?

A full-time employee is someone who is employed an average of at least 130 hours a month (in other words, at least thirty hours per week). You calculate this average by looking at a sample of an employee's work record over at least three months (but not more than twelve months). That sounds simple enough, but there's an additional complication.

If you have a large number of part-time employees, you need to determine how these add up. Do this by adding all the hours in a month worked by part-time employees and dividing that number by 130. This will give you the number of FTEs you employ. Add that number to the number of workers working more than 130 hours per month and you get your total number of FTE employees for purposes of determining the size of your company.

If, after making this calculation, you find that you have more than fifty full-time workers or FTEs, you can't use the SHOP marketplace to offer health insurance to your employees (keep in mind that in 2016, all SHOPs will be open to employers with up to 100 full-time workers or FTEs).

Do seasonal employees count?

Theoretically, no. The ACA says that you can use a "reasonable good faith interpretation" of the term "seasonal employee" in determining the size of your company and whether you can offer insurance through the SHOP exchange. To determine whether you'll be affected, contact the Department of Labor for more specific guidelines. Start here to get a better understanding of how the Department of Labor categorizes seasonal workers: *www.dol.gov/dol/topic/workhours /seasonalemployment.htm.*

How and where do I report to the government about the coverage I'm providing my employees?

You're required to report the cost of health coverage under a group insurance plan on the employee's W-2 form, Wage and Tax Statement, in Box 12, using code DD. For more information on reporting, go to *www.irs.gov/uac/Form-W-2-Reporting-of-Employer-Sponsored-Health -Coverage.*

PART 2

HOW TO SELECT THE RIGHT HEALTHCARE PLAN

Choosing the right insurance company and plan to meet your needs can seem overwhelming, especially if you don't have employer-sponsored health insurance. You may be tempted to just pick the plan with the lowest monthly premium or the one that promises the lowest out-of-pocket expenses. However, selecting the right health plan for you (and your family, if applicable) requires looking at a variety of factors, not just one number.

A simple rule of thumb: Until you understand exactly what the policy offers and are confident that it will suit your needs, don't buy it!

Since under the Affordable Care Act you can no longer be denied healthcare coverage if you have a preexisting condition, plans can't refuse to cover treatment for any such conditions. The only exception is if you have a grandfathered individual health insurance plan (see

Part 1). That consideration used to drive a lot of insurance-related decision-making, but it doesn't need to anymore.

In Part 2, you'll find tips that will help assist you in finding the plan that is best for you, as well as strategies for how to compare the different types of plans you may be selecting from during your search.

THE DIFFERENT TYPES OF HEALTHCARE PLANS

What is an HMO?

A Health Maintenance Organization, or HMO, is a type of group health insurance plan. An HMO is a managed-care plan that requires you to select a primary care physician (PCP) from the plan's list of contracted providers (their "network"). This PCP oversees all of your basic care. In general, you cannot see a specialist without a referral from your PCP and, in some cases, preauthorization from the insurance company. Specialists generally have to be in the network as well, or their charges may not be paid by the insurance company at all (or you may owe a larger percentage of the expense, called "going out-of-network"). You will also need to obtain preauthorization from the insurance company for certain medical procedures, even routine and common ones.

HMOs use this requirement to reduce healthcare expenses and control their costs. This is the most common type of health insurance plan, and most health insurance companies provide an HMO option. It also tends to be the least expensive kind of health insurance and the least flexible. However, it can be a good option if there is a sufficient variety of doctors and other healthcare providers in the network.

Is an HMO the right plan for me?

Before you run out and sign up for an HMO, please keep the following pros and cons in mind:

- Generally, you won't have to file a claim form for office visits or hospital stays. The insurance company is billed directly by the provider.
- HMOs focus on preventative medicine and may provide access to programs or specialists who will help you develop healthier habits.
- With most HMOs, you must stay in your network of doctors and medical facilities or risk having to pay the entire charge yourself.
- You may have to wait longer for an appointment than you would with some other forms of insurance (providers may be overbooked). You may also find that the time you can spend with your healthcare provider is strictly limited. For example, a healthcare provider may only be paid for a fifteen-minute follow-up visit for a common complaint (no matter how long it actually takes), meaning the provider is more likely to try to keep things brief.
- You will probably make a small copayment for each office visit.
- It can be difficult to get specialized care, and extremely expensive if you go outside the network for that care.
- Situations covered as emergency care are strictly limited. Problems that are urgent (a deep gash on your leg, for example) but are not life threatening may not be covered.
- Because of all the rules and expectations for providers, there may be a high turnover rate among them.

Your local state Insurance Department can provide you with a list of HMOs in your area, as well as general background information on which healthcare services are covered. Visit *www.naic.org/state_web_map.htm*.

If you are looking for the least expensive, simplest policy and rarely see your physician, this may be a good choice for you. However, if you have unusual medical needs or frequently need to see specialists, there may be a better option.

What is a PPO?

Preferred Provider Organizations (PPOs) are a type of managed-care health insurance plan. They are loosely organized groups of physicians, hospitals, and other healthcare providers who have agreed with an insurance company to provide healthcare for that insurer's customers at predetermined levels of reimbursement for specific services. The healthcare providers agree not to charge you (the insurance customer) for anything over that predetermined level. In other words, if the provider's normal fee for a particular service is $120, but they've agreed with the insurance company to charge $100 for the service, they can't then charge you the additional $20.

Unlike with an HMO, you don't need to choose a primary care physician, and generally you can see any healthcare provider within the network without a referral and without preauthorization from the insurance company.

Unfortunately, the numbers of physicians and hospitals who are in the network are generally limited, and are often given standards to follow regarding care; usually there is very little deviance from this standard treatment plan. You will have some flexibility with your healthcare decisions, and especially when selecting your providers (both inside and outside the network).

However, there is a definite financial incentive to remain within the network of PPO providers. For example, you will pay a higher percentage of the bill if you receive services from a hospital or doctor that is not part of the PPO network.

Unlike HMOs, PPOs do not require you to have authorization to go to a doctor outside their plan. If you prefer a little more flexibility in your choice of doctors, this may be the best choice for you. Keep in mind that every PPO may also vary slightly in policy, so be sure to study each one carefully.

What are the advantages and disadvantages of selecting a PPO?

There are definitely pros and cons to choosing a PPO. Here are some of the advantages:

- Your healthcare costs are usually relatively low when using providers within the PPO network. You will generally have a good sense of how much you will end up paying out of pocket for any particular problem or treatment.
- Unlike with an HMO, you can consult any doctor or specialist, including ones outside the plan, without getting preauthorization. Out-of-network visits are usually reimbursed at a lower rate than in-network visits. An exception is when there is no specialist of the type you need in the network. Then the insurance company will often cover the cost as if the provider were in-network (you will need to contact the insurance company to determine their policy about this).
- You don't have to see a primary care physician prior to scheduling an appointment with a specialist, and you don't need referrals or preauthorization for seeing a healthcare provider who is in the network.

But of course there are a few disadvantages as well:

- If you go outside the network, you will have to file claims with your insurance company and deal with whatever paperwork is required to substantiate the need for treatment.
- If you go out of the network, such as to see a provider you prefer, your costs will be significantly more expensive.
- Your copayments for office visits are usually larger than you would find with an HMO.
- You may need to pay an annual deductible. This is particularly relevant if you go out-of-network for care; in that case, you are normally responsible for meeting the deductible, which is usually several thousand dollars, before your PPO begins contributing to the cost of your care. After your deductible is met, you will still be required to pay a percentage of the cost (generally 10–40 percent). Your coinsurance percentage, as this is called, is higher if you use out-of-network providers than if you use in-network providers. Additionally, you may have to pay the difference between what your out-of-network provider charges and what your PPO has decided is "reasonable and customary" for the service. For example, if the out-of-network provider charges $175 for a service, and your PPO says that $125 is reasonable and customary, that is all they will allow, and they may pay only 70 percent of that fee (leaving you to pay the other 30 percent as your coinsurance). Additionally, you may end up responsible for paying the gap of $50 between $125 and $175.

How can I evaluate the quality of a particular PPO?

In order to determine if a particular PPO is right for you (or if you'd be better off choosing another option, such as an HMO), ask the following questions:

- Are the doctors, hospitals, and other healthcare providers you're already using in the network, or would you have to pay the out-of-network expenses to use them (or change to new providers)?
- Are the hospitals, doctors' offices, and other sites in the network conveniently located, or would you have to travel an unreasonable distance?
- If you need to see a specialist, do you need to get a referral or a preauthorization? If your specialist is out-of-network, does the answer change?
- Does the plan limit payment for emergency care? In what ways?
- What specific healthcare services are covered? For example, if you routinely see a chiropractor, you'll want to be sure that such services are covered in the plan.
- Are prevention services covered? What about mental health services?
- What are the limits on treatments? Are certain kinds of treatments not allowed?
- What is the monthly premium for the insurance, and how does this compare to other plans?
- Does the plan limit how much you will pay out of pocket annually?

- What are the copayments for specific services? Will you be responsible for coinsurance for in-network care?
- What is the cost of using out-of-network providers, including deductible and coinsurance?

Before making a decision, consider what your healthcare needs have been in the past. For example, if you need to see a lot of specialists, a PPO might be better than an HMO for you. However, if your specialist isn't in-network, the financial burden could be significantly greater than if you found a plan in which your specialist participates. You should know the financial costs to you of the various choices available.

What are Exclusive Provider Organizations (EPOs)?

In addition to the common managed-care plans (HMOs and PPOs), there are hybrid options that address some of the drawbacks of HMOs and PPOs. One of these hybrids is called an Exclusive Provider Organization (EPO) plan.

An EPO, like an HMO, has a network of contracted healthcare providers. However, you don't have to name a primary care physician or obtain a referral to see any provider in the network. In this way, the plan combines the cost-effectiveness of an HMO contracting with providers to provide services at previously agreed-upon levels of reimbursement with one of the benefits of a PPO, not having to get referrals to see specialists.

In addition, you don't have to file claim forms or deal with bills, but you do have to get preauthorization for certain medical treatments and services. This can be tricky because if you don't get the preauthorization, the plan won't pay for the services. If you go out-of-network for anything other than emergency care, it is likely that the insurance company will not pay.

An EPO is generally lower-cost than a traditional PPO, with lower monthly premiums and lower copayments and coinsurance, but you will need to stay in-network to get the biggest benefit from the plan.

What is a Point of Service (POS) plan?

A POS plan is a type of managed-care plan that includes elements of both PPOs and HMOs. Like an HMO, you usually have to select a primary care physician who will be responsible for your basic care. You will also need to get referrals in order to see specialists. However, the plan will reimburse for visits to providers outside your network (which is like a PPO but unlike an HMO). Out-of-network visits are covered at a lesser rate than in-network visits, meaning you might have to make a larger copayment, pay a larger percent for coinsurance, and pay an annual deductible for out-of-network care. The rules may vary depending on the provider and treatment. As with a PPO, for any out-of-network care, you'll be responsible for filing claims and dealing with paperwork.

What are High-Deductible Health Plans?

A High-Deductible Health Plan (HDHP) is a type of insurance with (not surprisingly) a high deductible. With a few exceptions, none of your medical expenses are met until after you've paid the entire deductible out of pocket. Most of these plans are going away because the ACA limits how high the deductible can be on a conforming plan. However, a number of high-deductible plans have been grandfathered in, so if you're already on one, you may be able to keep it.

Typically, a high-deductible plan would work best for someone who has very limited healthcare needs and can pay out of pocket for most routine healthcare. A high-deductible policy is less expensive than other types of insurance.

People often combine high-deductible insurance plans with a Health Insurance Account or a Flexible Spending Account, which means they use pretax income to pay the medical expenses the high-deductible plan does not pay.

What is a health savings account (HSA)?

A health savings account (HSA) is used in connection with high-deductible health insurance plans. You contribute a certain amount of your pretax (and tax-free) income to your HSA and use it to pay unreimbursed medical expenses. These accounts are generally offered by your employer. (An MSA, or medical savings account, is a similar plan intended for use by self-employed individuals and small business owners.) However, you own and control the account.

The money in the account is not taxed and you can use the money without penalty to pay qualified medical expenses (expenses must be for the beneficiary of the account, like you and your family—you can't use it to pay off your neighbor's dental bill). You can find out more about qualified medical expenses at *www.irs.gov/publications /p502/index.html.*

There are limits to how much you can contribute to an HSA each year as well as other rules you must follow about setting up an

HSA. More information about that can be found here: *www.irs.gov/ publications/p969/ar02.html*

If you don't spend all the money you've accumulated in your HSA during a given year, the money will roll over and be available for expenses incurred in future years. Once you reach retirement age, you may be able to use the assets of your HSA for retirement expenses (not just medical expenses), subject to ordinary income tax.

If, before retirement, you make withdrawals from your HSA to pay for nonmedical purposes, the funds are taxed and you'll pay a penalty; this is similar to what would happen if you withdrew money early from an IRA.

If you die, your spouse can use the money in your HSA to pay for his/her qualifying medical expenses. Be aware that different states have additional rules about the use of HSAs. You can find out more about that here: *www.healthinsurancefinders.com/cr_state_department_ of_insurance.html*.

What is a flexible spending account (FSA)?

A flexible spending account is similar to a health savings account in that you can use the pretax dollars to pay for unreimbursed medical expenses. These are offered through your employer, who sets up certain rules about them (in addition to the rules and limits the government puts on them, including a cap on contributions). Unlike an HSA, you don't have to be on a qualifying high-deductible health insurance plan in order to start and fund an FSA. You can find out more about the requirements and limits of an FSA by going to *www*

.irs.gov and downloading Publication 969, which explains various tax-favored health plans.

Contributions to your FSA are made pretax and do not incur a tax liability. If you know you have certain fixed medical expenses every year (such as medication or psychiatric expenses) that are not covered by your health insurance plan, an FSA can be a smart way to save a little money.

Unfortunately, when it comes to FSAs, unlike an HSA, if you do not use the funds in your FSA by the end of the year, you will lose them so you will want to be sure you don't over-save in this account. FSA holders often try to use their FSA funds at the end of the year by stocking up on medications, medical equipment (such as bandages), and the types of visits that insurance usually doesn't cover (such as dental or vision exams). You cannot pay insurance premiums out of your FSA.

MEDICAID, MEDICARE, AND OTHER GOVERNMENT PROGRAMS

What is Medicaid?

Medicaid is a state- and federal-funded government program that provides health coverage for people who meet certain established income and resource levels. Coverage varies by state, and under the ACA many states have expanded who is eligible for Medicaid. Some of the basic benefits that the states must include are:

- Basic hospital care
- Basic physician services
- Basic laboratory and radiology services
- Basic nursing service
- Family planning services
- Special health screening for children
- Care in nursing facilities and for home-based services

States may also offer additional benefits, such as transportation to and from medical appointments, and additional services such as physical therapy and rehabilitation.

For more information on Medicaid services, and to find out if you qualify, visit *www.medicaid.gov*.

If I don't qualify for Medicaid, are there other programs that can assist me?

Yes! Just because you don't qualify for Medicaid doesn't mean there are no state funds available for you and your family. Double check with your state to see what new programs it may be offering.

This may take a little research, but a good place to start is your state's Department of Health (*www.medicaid.gov/Medicaid-CHIP -Program-Information/By-State/By-State.html*).

An example of one of these state and federally funded programs is the State Children's Health Insurance Program (SCHIP). This program is generally for low-income families who do not have health insurance for their children under the age of nineteen. Each state determines the design of its program, eligibility groups, benefit packages, payment levels for coverage, and administrative and operating procedures.

In most states, those who qualify for benefits pay little or no cost. This type of insurance generally pays for doctor visits, immunizations, hospitalizations, and emergency room visits. In other states, this may cover women who are pregnant. For contact information for your state and for specific information on CHIP, go to *www.insure kidsnow.gov.*

In addition, if you do not qualify for Medicaid this year, be sure to check again next year. Many states are expanding their Medicaid programs.

What is Medicare, and am I eligible?

Medicare is a health insurance program designed for older citizens. You do not have to meet income limits in order to qualify for the program. There are two parts, Part A and Part B, which are (roughly) hospital services (Part A) and other healthcare services, such as outpatient doctors' visits (Part B).

Medicare is not just for people who are sixty-five and older. You are eligible for Medicare Part A if:

- Your spouse is getting (or eligible for) retirement benefits from Social Security or Railroad Retirement
- You are under sixty-five and getting Social Security Disability Insurance (SSDI) or Railroad Retirement disability benefits (although there might be a twenty-four-month waiting period for people in this category)
- You are under sixty-five years of age with end-stage renal disease (ESRD) and you and your spouse have met the Medicare work requirement

To qualify for Medicare, you must have been employed for a certain number of years. To find out if you're eligible and how much premiums will cost, call 1-800-Medicare or 1-800-633-4227 or go to *www* *.medicare.gov/eligibilitypremiumcalc/*.

What is Social Security Disability Insurance?

Social Security Disability Insurance (SSDI) provides you with income if illness or injury prevents you from being able to work for an extended period of time. To qualify for SSDI, you must have worked a certain number of years. If you've never worked, or haven't worked for long enough, you may qualify for Supplemental Security Income (SSI) instead.

This is an important but often overlooked form of insurance. To find out if you qualify and to learn about possible benefits, go to *www* *.ssa.gov/pubs/10029.html*.

To receive benefits, you'll have to get an official determination from the Social Security Administration. You can find the closest Social Security Office near you by going to *secure.ssa.gov/ICON/main.jsp*. You can complete an online application at *www.ssa.gov/pgm/disability.htm*.

Figuring out if you're eligible for disability compensation from the government (and, if so, how much) can be complicated. One resource that can help is The National Organization of Social Security Claimants' Representatives (NOSSCR), which is an association of attorneys who are experts on the disability determination process. You can learn more about them (and contact them) on their website, *www.nosscr.org*.

To make the determination process easier, you'll need to have the following information (and documentation):

- The date your disability started.
- Copies of your medical records.
- Any notes you or a companion made about your symptoms when you visited a doctor. It helps if such notes are specific and include things like the date of the doctor's visit and any treatment the doctor suggested or prescribed.
- Any notes or documents giving dates when you were sick or had other health problems, particularly if you had to miss work because of your disability.
- A Social Security Administration application.

Please remember that besides this insurance, there are other possible sources of income if you are or become disabled. Workers' compensation provides benefits if the illness or injury is work-related; civil service disability covers federal or state government workers; and automobile insurance may pay benefits if the disability results from an automobile accident.

The National Disability Rights Network (*www.ndrn.org*) may be able to help you understand what disability programs are available in your state.

If I don't qualify for Social Security Disability Insurance, are there other options available to me?

Yes! You can purchase short-term and long-term disability insurance. This is often available through your employer. If you're self-employed, you may be able to purchase these types of insurance through a broker.

Both types of insurance are intended to help replace some percentage of your income should you be unable to work owing to a disability. As the name implies, short-term disability insurance is intended for temporary, short-term disabilities (such as a broken leg that makes it impossible for you to continue working as a forklift driver but from which you will eventually recover). Long-term disability is for, predictably, disabilities from which you will take significantly longer to recover or that are permanent.

Most plans require a waiting period before the benefit kicks in. You will receive typically from 50 to 70 percent of your usual pay.

Some policies pay benefits only if you can't perform your usual job duties while others pay only if you cannot engage in any type of gainful employment. Make sure that you know the insurer's definition of disability. Some policies pay only for accidents, but it's important to be insured for illness, too. Be sure, as you evaluate policies, that both accident and illness are covered.

Benefits may be payable for a period ranging anywhere from one year to a lifetime. Since disability benefits replace income, most people do not need benefits beyond their working years. It's generally wise to insure yourself to at least age sixty-five, since a lengthy disability threatens financial security much more than a short disability.

RESEARCHING YOUR OPTIONS FOR HEALTH INSURANCE

I don't even know where to start! How do I begin my search?

You should know specifically what you want and need from your health insurance, which in itself may require some thought. For example, if you're young, healthy, and single, you'll probably make a different choice from someone who is older, has a family to cover, and has a chronic condition that needs special care.

Once you have an idea of your needs, your next step is to find out what plans are available in your state of residency.

Ask yourself these questions:

- Do you want coverage for your whole family, or just yourself?
- Are you concerned with preventive care and checkups?
- Are you comfortable in a managed-care setting that might restrict your choice somewhat but give you broad coverage and convenience?

How can I find out what a plan will cost?

You can compare plans in the insurance exchanges by going to *www .healthcare.gov* and checking out the available options. A quick way to get a reasonable guess as to what your premiums will be (in general, not tied to a specific plan) is to use the calculator at *http://laborcenter .berkeley.edu/healthpolicy/calculator/*.

Another option is to check out prices of plans offered by various insurance companies by going to that company's website and exploring the different options offered. Some insurance companies, such as Blue Cross/Blue Shield, have all of their plans and benefits listed on their website, making it easier to compare. Use the information you find on the Internet as preliminary research material, then call the company and ask them to elaborate on what you have learned.

I would also recommend locating your state insurance commissioner in the department of insurance for more information. Go to *www .naic.org* and find the "States and Jurisdiction Map" tab at the top of the page. Then click on your state on the map of the United States. This will lead you to the website of your state's insurance commissioner, where you can find out a lot about what's happening in insurance-related issues. You never know what new plans are coming out in your area, as well as new rules that may change the benefits of your current plan.

Your state insurance website may include a list of companies selling individual coverage in your state, including those that aren't handled by brokers. The insurance department may provide shopping tips for your state, as well as insurance-company complaint records.

How do I compare plans?

Using the insurance exchange website (*www.healthcare.gov*), you can compare various policies available in your state. Your first step is to look for the benefits summary or outline of coverage given for each plan. This may include the description of policy benefits, exclusions, and provisions that make it easier to understand a particular policy and compare it with others.

Take the time to evaluate each plan's coverage and features, taking into account exclusions, limitations, and the freedom to choose healthcare providers. Find out how much you'll end up paying out of pocket in the form of copayments, coinsurance, and deductibles, because even relatively small amounts of money can add up if you make frequent visits to your doctor.

When comparing health insurance plans, consider how much the plan pays for each of the following types of services (and consider how likely you are to need them):

- Inpatient hospital services
- Outpatient surgery
- Inpatient physician visits
- Office visits to various healthcare providers
- Skilled nursing care
- Prescription drugs
- Radiology and other diagnostic tests
- Mental healthcare
- Drug and alcohol abuse treatment
- Home healthcare visits
- Rehabilitation facility care
- Physical therapy and speech therapy
- Maternity care
- Hospice care
- Chiropractic treatment
- Preventive care and checkups
- Well-baby care
- Dental care
- Other covered services

If you get healthcare coverage at work, or through a trade or professional association or a union, you are almost certainly enrolled under a group contract. Generally, the contract is between the group and the insurer, and your employer has done comparison-shopping before offering the plan to the employees. Nevertheless, while some employers only offer one plan, some offer more than one. Compare your potential plans carefully!

What are specific facts I should consider when comparing plans?

Here are some important questions to ask so that you can be sure the plan you pick will work best for you (and your family, if you have one).

- How much is the premium? When will it be paid (every month, quarter, or year)?
- Are there any medical service limits, exclusions, or preexisting conditions that will affect you or your family? (This may occur with a grandfathered plan.)
- What types of preauthorization or certification procedures are required?
- Are there any discounts available for good health or healthy behaviors (e.g., nonsmoker)?
- How much is the annual deductible (per person and per family)?
- What is the coinsurance percentage?
- What is the copay per office visit?
- What is the copay and/or percentage of coinsurance for wellness care (includes well-baby care, annual eye exam, physical, etc.)?

- What is the percentage of copay and/or coinsurance for inpatient hospital care?

Having specific answers to these questions will help you select the best plan for your needs and your pocketbook.

What if I'm not sure whether a benefit is covered?

It's important that you understand the benefits of a particular plan and are sure that it is the right one for you and your family. If you have questions about coverage that you can't answer by looking at the benefits summary or outline of coverage, call the insurance company and have them clarify it. Don't let them brush you off and say, "Look in your benefits information on our website."

If you feel the answer was incomplete, ask to speak to a supervisor and be sure to document the names and contact information of every person to whom you speak, just in case you need to reference them later on.

I have a pretty good idea of the type of plan I want. Now what?

Your next step is to confirm that the policy you're considering is the right one for you. Keep in mind that you may qualify for a government plan such as Medicare or Medicaid, so it may make sense to check your eligibility for those programs before you go too much further. Since income and other eligibility rules change from time to time, it's smart to check at least occasionally, especially if you've had a change in income or other circumstances, such as a change in your household size.

If Medicaid or Medicare are not possibilities for you, then the next step is to read the actual policy for the insurance plan you're thinking of buying. Remember you want to read the *policy*, not just the summary of benefits. Make sure you understand all of its provisions. Looking over the marketing or sales literature is no substitute for reading the actual policy. You should be able to request one directly from the insurance company (their website should show you how to do this).

Some companies won't provide the complete policy until you purchase the insurance. In that case, go to the website and use the tools there to examine as much as you can about the plan. For instance, most insurance companies will list participating providers on their websites. Others will provide in-depth information about their wellness plans. Be sure to take this extra step of exploring the plan you're considering as completely as possible.

As you read the policy (or explore the website), consider the following factors:

- What is your medical history? Do you have cancer or diabetes in your family? At what age were your family members diagnosed with the ailment? What was their treatment regime? Will the insurance you're considering be the best one for these types of potential problems?
- How many times a year do you get sick? What are the illnesses and what are the best treatments for you? Will this insurance plan address those needs?
- Do you plan on having a family this year? Is it possible you might have a high-risk pregnancy? If so, what does the policy say about maternity coverage?

- Are you on any medications such as birth control or heart medication? Do you take antibiotics when you get sick? How often do you take this medication, and in what quantity? Are there certain medications you cannot live without, or can you easily substitute a generic if that is all the health plan offers? Check out the prescription benefit and compare it with your needs.
- Ask friends with similar health conditions what they liked and did not like about their health insurance.
- Are there certain providers you prefer, such as an ob-gyn whom you have been going to for years, a cardiologist who knows your family's heart health history, a certain pharmacy you prefer, or even a diagnostic center you just can't part with? Will you still be able to use these providers on the plan you're considering?

Good insurance agents and good insurance companies want you to know what you are buying. Don't be afraid to ask your benefits manager, insurance agent, or insurance company to explain anything that is unclear.

I need a plan that will work for my family, not just me. What else do I need to consider?

Here are some questions you should ask before selecting a plan for your family.

- How is the overall health of your family?
- Have there been any major medical changes within your family, and what are they?
- What medications do you and your family members need, and which ones can you get the generics for?
- Are there any treatments that your family members would need covered, such as infusions or physical therapy?
- Does anyone in the family use durable medical equipment such as crutches or walkers?
- What emergency room would you prefer to go to in case of an emergency?

I am trying to compare various plans, but I'm confused. One plan has my doctor, but another plan has a lower deductible. What now?

You may want to make a list of the main features of two or three plans that you're considering and rate them against each other. To do this, write down the answers to your questions for each of the plans. For example, one question might be, does your primary care physician participate in a certain plan? You can look up the answer and then note it for each plan.

You might find that one policy has your hospital included in it, but your preferred doctor is not, while your doctor is included in another policy but your preferred hospital is not. In a case like that, you need to prioritize: What's most important to you—being able to see your doctor in-network, or being able to go to your preferred hospital?

If you're relatively healthy and don't anticipate requiring much medical care in the near future, you may find it makes sense to pick a low-cost policy that will cover you in case something unexpected comes up. But if you have a chronic condition that has to be managed, concerns such as how easy it is to see specialists will get higher priority.

How can I find out if my doctor is in an insurance company's network?

Many insurance companies provide lists of their in-network providers on their websites. Some will send this information if you request it before you purchase a policy. Others will only disclose it once you have purchased a policy.

If you're choosing a plan in large part because your healthcare provider accepts the plan, call your healthcare provider and confirm that he or she is still participating before you enroll in the plan. Providers occasionally choose to stop participating in certain insurance plans and insurance companies don't always immediately update their provider lists.

If your provider is not included, you may want to find out if they'll consider joining the plan before making a final decision.

How can I find out if the medications I take are on the plan?

Many insurance companies include their formularies (lists of drugs for which they provide some amount of reimbursement) on their websites. Some will send this information if you request it before you purchase a policy. Others will only disclose it once you have purchased a policy.

The best way to know if your medications are covered is to ask your health insurance provider. Be sure to get the information in writing. Do not rely on what you are told over the phone.

Once you enroll in a plan, you should receive a booklet that describes the formulary and lists all of the approved medications, along with an explanation of the various copayments. If you have not received a formulary, call the customer service number on your drug card to request one.

Keep in mind that is not unusual for an insurance plan to include your providers, but maybe not the prescriptions you prefer. Make a list of what you can and cannot live without when deciding what plan to choose.

However, if you're happy with most of the plan but find it does not cover medications you need, ask your prescribing physician if there is a generic version of the medication or a comparable substitute. The easiest way to go about this is to bring the list of medications to your next appointment, go over them with your doctor, and agree on a possible treatment/prescription plan. Be sure you consider not only your daily medications, but medications you prefer if you become ill, such as antibiotics.

I've decided on the plan I want. How can I be sure the company will deliver on their promises?

One way you can evaluate a company is to look for its rating. There are several websites that grade insurance companies in your area. The National Committee for Quality Assurance, whose focus is to "measure the quality of America's Health Care," offers an array of information on health insurance policies in your area at *www.reportcard.ncqa .org/plan/external/plansearch.aspx*.

Consumer Reports also rates insurance companies. Check out their website at *www.consumerreports.org*.

In addition, you may have a specific period of time to return the policy and get your money back if it does not meet your needs. This is called the "free look." You might want to try out the company's customer service at this time and see if it meets your expectations by calling them with a claims or appeals question to see how they handle the situation. If they transfer you to several other departments, keep you on hold, or don't give you clear answers, you might want to consider another plan. You may also want to call a few doctors on the plan to be sure the ones listed are still accepting new patients or are not about to drop the policy.

Always remember that you can switch policies during your open enrollment period, so even if you miss the free-look period, you're not locked in forever.

Can you tell me more about what "free look" means when it comes to my health insurance plan?

Many people aren't aware that this rule exists, but it's extremely valuable. It's similar to "right to rescind" laws that were put in place to help people cancel a sale and get their money back if they regret certain kinds of purchases or find them other than as advertised.

Depending on what state you live in, most health insurance companies are required to provide you with at least a ten-day free look at your policy. Basically what this means is that you have ten (or more) days from the receipt of your policy document to return the policy and get your money back if it does not meet your needs.

Your request must be made in writing. Be sure you can provide proof of the date of receipt of the policy document. This free-look period allows you to go through the terms and conditions of the policy and reverse the purchase decision if you find it unsuitable.

Many insurers provide free-look forms, which must be downloaded from their website and filled out in order to start the process. If you decide to cancel your policy within the free-look period, you will need to find out the health insurance company's protocol. Most of them require that you provide the date of receipt of the policy document, agent information (if any), the reason for cancellation/change, your address, and sometimes your bank information (depending on how you paid your first month's premium).

Some of the state health insurance commissioners recently have ruled against allowing the free-look period when it comes to the newer individual Marketplace policies under the ACA. If you are unsure of the rules behind the free-look period in your state, visit *www.naic.org/state_web_map.htm* to find out if you can take advantage of the free-look period *before* fully committing to a health insurance plan. Otherwise, you may be stuck with it until the next open enrollment period.

If it turns out my plan doesn't suit my needs, when and how can I switch plans?

In general, you have to wait for the next open enrollment period. The actual date of this period for people using the healthcare insurance exchanges will occur at different times in the next few years (although it will always start toward the end of the calendar year). For open enrollment periods after that, visit *www.healthcare.gov* and search "open enrollment."

My advice is to take notes on what you did not like about your current plan, as well as what you did like. Remember, you have to live with the plan you choose for a year, which should be more than enough time to figure out what you need from a health insurance plan. As you approach the open enrollment period, present any questions or issues to your current health insurer or human resources (HR) department at work, and be sure not to select a plan that may present the same problems you have in your current plan. You might be surprised to find that some health insurers will actually go the extra mile to make changes to keep their customers happy, especially if they are part of a larger organization and the company is receiving multiple complaints on the same issue. The same goes for the HR department, which is in the hot seat for choosing its company's health insurance. If the company wants to keep its employees happy and is receiving complaints about a plan, they may well consider changing it for all employees during the next open enrollment period.

If you have a life event that affects your insurance such as getting married, having or adopting a child, permanently moving to a new area that offers different health plan options, or losing other health coverage due to a job loss, divorce, loss of eligibility for Medicaid or CHIP, expiration of COBRA coverage, or a health plan being decertified, you can choose a new health insurance plan even if the event takes place outside the open enrollment period.

If you drop your plan without replacing it, you run the risk of having to pay a penalty for the months you are not covered. If you lose your coverage because you do not have minimum essential coverage (described in Part 1 in the section "Basic Terminology"), decided not to pay your premiums, or if you simply forgot, you may be stuck paying a penalty. However, if you already enrolled in Marketplace coverage and have a change in income or household status that affects your tax credit eligibility or cost-sharing reductions, you may not be subject to a penalty.

One important fact to remember is if you have a qualifying life event as mentioned previously, you must report this change within thirty days to your insurance or the Marketplace. You will then have approximately sixty days from the date of your life-changing event to select and enroll in a new plan (assuming that's necessary).

If you recently had a baby, please note that most health insurances will cover infants automatically from the moment they are born (although not all plans do); however, to continue coverage, you must add your newborn to the plan immediately. Otherwise, your infant will lose coverage after thirty days. It is best to call your health insurance provider at least a few weeks before your due date to verify the protocol. Be sure to notify them if you are expecting multiple births. You don't want to be scrambling to find coverage once your child/children are born.

I don't have time to do all this research myself. Do I have any options?

Finding a plan that works to your advantage on your own can be a long and tedious process, which is why some people opt to have someone else do the research for them. While some use an insurance agent or salesperson, these people generally work for one specific insurance company. A broker, on the other hand, works with a broad range of companies and can help explain what you are getting from your insurance, as well as make sure that you and your family are on the best plan for your needs. Brokers not only will help you shop for price, they'll also know if a company has a reputation for raising premiums or hassling policyholders who file claims.

If your potential insurance broker makes it seem complicated and too difficult to understand, run for the hills. Usually, there is a reason they are being unclear: They have something to hide. Your insurance information should be crystal clear and very simple to understand. After all, your healthcare premium is usually the second or third largest monthly payment you will be making, next to your home and car, so choose wisely.

Don't let an insurance agent or broker tell you what you need; instead, make them match your needs. Read the fine print in every plan you're considering and ask questions. Just because the broker tells you that a liver transplant is covered does not make him responsible if it turns out to not be covered. Remember to document (in writing) everything you discuss with the broker.

Using a broker sounds good to me. Where can I find one?

Finding a broker can be difficult, but once you find one you are comfortable with, you won't have to worry about keeping up with your ever-changing health insurance policy. Many life- and auto-insurance agents don't deal in health insurance because the rules are complicated and the commissions are low. However, they may be able to refer you to a specialist.

The National Association of Health Underwriters (*www.nahu.org*) or your local state commissioner may be able to put you in touch with a reputable broker in your area. You want to find a broker who has a large book (that is, works with a wide variety of companies), is someone you trust, and who has sufficient experience to know what policies are best for your individual needs. The right broker can save you a lot of time and headache in the future.

Once I choose my plan, can I just set it and forget it?

No. Evaluate your health plan every year. Don't sign up for the same health plan year after year simply because it's convenient. Look into new plans that are offered and be sure you understand any changes that have occurred with your current plan. These days, the real differences lie in the plans' copays and deductibles, not the premiums.

To figure out which option is best for you, estimate what your total annual costs will be under each plan, depending on your family's situation and medical needs. If your personal situation has changed, your insurance plan may need to change, too. So, ask yourself if any of the following have occurred:

- Did you recently get married?
- Did you recently have children?
- Are you taking care of your parents?
- Did your doctor drop the plan you were in?
- Is your plan covering necessary screening procedures?
- Most important, are you just not satisfied with your current health plan?

This is your opportunity to reevaluate the plan you're in and switch to a better plan if you need to. Keep track of the open season each year and use the opportunity to change plans if necessary.

PART 3

USING YOUR HEALTH INSURANCE BENEFITS WISELY

For some people, the ACA allows them to get medical care they've been neglecting for a while because they didn't have insurance before or their insurance was inadequate. For others, choosing a new health insurance plan means finding a new doctor or other healthcare providers. In both cases, you may have a lot of decisions to make!

Having good health insurance is great news, but using it wisely can be a bit of a challenge. This part has been written to help you use your health insurance most effectively, by helping you understand how to get the best care possible for yourself and your family.

In this part, we'll explore how to find the right doctor for you, including how to research a doctor's background and understand what his or her credentials mean; how to change doctors if you need; what you should do to get the most out of a visit to your doctor; how to get second opinions; and how to be a wise consumer of healthcare.

We'll also talk about how to push back when a doctor recommends tests that may be unnecessary, and we'll discuss what types of testing you should expect to take during routine screenings (and those tests of which to be wary).

CHOOSING A DOCTOR

My new insurance plan requires me to choose a primary care physician, and the doctor I've been going to isn't on the plan. Why do I need a primary care physician?

Your primary care physician should be someone who will coordinate and oversee your overall medical care, referring you to a specialist only if needed. It is not usually a good idea to consult specialists for every problem you have. Specialists sometimes order unnecessary tests (which can be expensive and painful) to rule out rare diseases (after all, they are specialists, and they cannot afford to overlook any possibility, however remote it may be, while making a diagnosis).

Ideally, a primary care doctor can offer you the following benefits:

- *A good starting point in the healthcare system.* Whatever your concern or problem may be, your primary care doctor will be able to either treat it or determine precisely when and where to send you for specialized help. In either case, you have the distinct advantage of a physician's expertise, and any trips through the medical maze will be less confusing for you—and less of a hassle.
- *Preventive healthcare.* Your primary care doctor can help you with disease prevention, as well as provide prompt intervention during any illness.

- *Continuity of care.* You and your doctor can develop and sustain an ongoing health partnership. He/she will get to know your concerns, and you won't have to repeat your history each time you fall ill or need treatment. Your primary care doctor will know you as well as any chronic problems or potential troubles you may be facing. He/she will also be familiar with your family history.
- *One-stop shopping.* You can consult the same doctor for a variety of conditions, and often, he can treat both you and your family. Your family doctor can take you and your family through pregnancy, childbirth, and childcare, thus instilling the concept of good health at an early age.
- *Lower cost and convenience.* Primary care doctors generally serve large populations of patients, so they encounter and become familiar with managing the most common medical maladies. They have been trained to diagnose and treat a wide range of conditions cost-effectively. Further, in most cases, it's easier to gain access to a primary care doctor than a specialist, since general practices are usually geared up for maximum efficiency.

Okay, I'll choose a primary care physician. Where do I start?

Many insurance companies require that you have a primary care doctor—a physician who can serve as the gatekeeper for your referrals, take care of basic medical needs, carry out regular checkups, and treat common illnesses. If you're already in a health plan, your choices may be limited to doctors who participate in the plan. Be sure you have an accurate and updated in-network provider list from your insurer.

If you have a doctor in mind (for example, someone a friend has recommended), call the doctor and make sure he or she is accepting new patients.

Unfortunately, a good doctor may not have room to add a new patient. If the doctor is not accepting new patients, ask for a recommendation. By using a referral from a doctor who is not accepting new patients, you might find a hidden gem. A good doctor will almost never recommend a bad doctor, because his reputation is at stake, and news of a bad doctor can spread very fast throughout the medical community, as well as the general public. The doctor who recommends a bad doctor will be questioned.

I don't have anyone in mind. Now what? Can't I just wait till I need to see someone for a problem?

Start looking for a doctor before you need one! This statement may seem paradoxical, but finding the right doctor when you are ill becomes much more difficult, because of the stress of the illness as well as the pressure of time.

When you are beginning your search, your first step should be to ask your friends for recommendations. Another good source of referrals can be nurses and other medical staff.

Nurses are always happy to help you choose a doctor and will not only recommend one who is competent, but also one with whom they like working. To you, this translates into a doctor who has good bedside manners. If you have an acquaintance or colleague who is a doctor, seek his or her advice as well.

A great resource is *www.vitals.com*. It makes finding a doctor like buying a plane ticket or a car. This website pools together various resources of information including affiliations, qualifications, practice specialties, cost, and even interests. The site grades them with a special algorithm along with written reviews. You can learn a good deal about the doctor and his or her practice, even before you actually meet, by merely checking out what other people have written.

I have the names of some doctors who come highly recommended, but how do I decide which is the right one for me?

Once you have a list of doctors who may meet your needs, it's time for the next step. What makes a good doctor *for you?* This is a very personal decision, so think about what you want and need. A few ideas are listed to follow. Add your own to create a list that will help you choose a doctor who is right for you.

For example, if your number one concern is that your doctor is highly rated by a consumer group, you will want to find out who did the ratings and if the information is reliable. Who collected it? Does the group judging the rankings have something to gain from rating doctors a certain way?

You may feel that your doctor needs to have experience with your condition(s). Research shows that doctors who have a lot of experience with a condition tend to have better success with it. If this is a major concern to you, your research should emphasize this.

A key thing to keep in mind is not all doctors have privileges at the hospital of your choice. Be sure to check if a doctor is permitted to practice at your hospital. Ask the office staff and double check with the hospital to be sure the doctor still has these privileges.

As explained before, your doctor should be in your insurance plan to avoid major charges. Keep in mind that doctors' busy schedules may keep them from realizing that they were dropped by an insurance plan. Be sure to check with not only the doctor's staff but with your insurance plan. You don't want to get into a situation where you love the doctor, but a month later, he does not accept your insurance, or your insurance does not accept your doctor.

What are some questions I can ask before making a final decision about a doctor?

Consider what's important to you, such as weekend office hours or quick response to calls. You might also want to ask who covers for the doctor when he or she is not available. Does the doctor have policies regarding how appointments are canceled? How long does it take to get an appointment? Does that change if your problem is urgent?

Many of these questions can be asked of the office staff, and some can be asked of the doctor during an initial consultation. Remember that you can usually change your primary care physician without any problem as long as you notify your insurance company that you've done so. So if you find out that the person you've chosen really isn't right for you, you can try again.

Look at the Appendix, "Questions to Ask Your Potential Doctor," for more information about how to screen for the right provider.

I'm not about to select a doctor based on a friend's recommendation and a couple of questions! How do I *really* research a doctor's background?

Keep in mind that not every doctor has the same type of training and experience, even those within the same specialty, especially in today's healthcare environment. In addition, no doctor will tell you outright whether he or she has been disciplined or had any malpractice judgments issued. The only way to find out is to research the doctor yourself.

The Internet is loaded with sites that claim to have information about doctors' credentials; however, you want to make sure you get more than just a doctor's license number and contact information.

For more comprehensive information, consider contacting the following sources:

- *Your local courthouse.* Many medical malpractice cases are settled before they go to trial. With a little digging you can find detailed information on the type of case it was and by reading the court documents, find out if it was a frivolous case by your standards or if it was something to be more concerned about.
- *Your state medical board.* They should have a record of complaints or disciplinary actions taken against the doctor. The state medical boards or state medical licensure is usually located in the Department of Health in your state. They should have up to date records of every doctor practicing legally, as well as those practicing on a pending license. To

obtain contact information for all the state medical boards go to *www.docboard.org.*

- *Your state department of insurance.* It's a good idea to check with this department to see if the doctor has any complaints against him or her, but remember that not all departments of insurance accept complaints. Find your state department of insurance here: *www.naic.org/state_web_map.htm.*
- *The American Board of Medical Specialties (ABMS).* This nonprofit organization includes twenty-four medical specialty boards. By checking online at *www.abms.org,* you can find out if your doctor is board-certified, which means he or she has completed a training program in a specialty and has passed some rigorous exams. Or call the ABMS at 1-866-275-2267. You can also check on your doctor's certification by going to *www.certifacts.org.* Remember that a primary care physician may be certified in a specialty.

Also, don't be afraid to ask health insurance plans and medical offices for information on their doctors' training and experience. They may have more information than you think.

The more research you conduct into this background, the more it will increase your chances of finding a healthcare provider who will satisfy your medical needs.

Investigate in advance, because it is always easier to cancel a first appointment than break off an established relationship with a doctor. When choosing a doctor, remember: it is your responsibility as the patient to make sure the doctor is an active participant in your healthcare plan. If this is assumed or overlooked, you may end up with a large unnecessary bill or suboptimal care.

What else do I need to consider when investigating a doctor's background?

Here are some basic, but important, criteria to find experienced, well-trained physicians:

- Make sure you chose a specialist who is board-certified in his or her respective field of specialty.
- Make sure no disciplinary actions have been instituted against the doctor.
- Look closely at malpractice judgments and how many have been brought against the doctor. (More than three is not good.)
- Find out if the doctor is fellowship-trained in his or her specialty field. This is usually a good sign.
- The more hospital affiliations or membership affiliations, the better. Hospitals vet their doctors before allowing them privileges.
- Check to see if the doctor has been practicing medicine for five years or more. Newer doctors make more mistakes.
- If the doctor has teaching responsibilities at any hospitals or other medical institutions, it's a very good sign.
- Find out how much of the doctor's practice focuses on the medical condition you have (or the surgery you need).
- Find out if the doctor has any awards, or is involved in his or her community. This generally means the doctor is well regarded.
- Listen to what other people in the community say about the doctor.

Which credentials should I look for?

Along with a background check, you should look at a doctor's credentials. While many of us tend to be overawed by a long list of letters after the doctor's name, you need to remember that not all of them are legitimate degrees, and if they are, the extra letters may not have any real meaning (as far as your health is concerned).

Some healthcare providers without an MD will call themselves "doctor" to give the impression that they have an MD or have been to medical school in the United States, when they actually have not. Someone who received his or her medical degree from another country may have gone through a different training program than a doctor educated in the United States. Some of these overseas programs are less rigorous than those found in the States.

The United States has certain standards that medical students from other countries must meet in order to practice in this country. If the doctor does not pass these tests, he or she may only be granted a limited license and have to take extra courses to bring him or her up to speed with U.S. practices.

Some people may not feel it is necessary to obtain these extra certification qualifications and practice general medicine. Be careful, as some doctors may be practicing advanced medicine without the extra certification.

Many doctors will use the acronyms FACP (Medicine), FACS (Surgery), FACG (Gastroenterology), FRCP (UK), MRCP (UK), etc., after their degree. These are often not educational qualifications, but represent awards bestowed upon the physician for years of service, teaching, or membership in a certain medical group. They don't necessarily have any bearing on the doctor's ability to take good care of you!

Many magazines produce "top doc" articles, but use discretion when considering them in your research. Most of these types of articles aren't well researched and depend on surveys that may have little to do with a doctor's true abilities.

The most important qualification of your physician is the quality of training he or she received after medical school. The location of the doctor's internship, residency, fellowship, and advanced fellowship can often mean more than where a doctor received his or her degree. Publications are also a significant factor. It is very important to know your doctor's educational and training background and check his or her credentials. After all, this is your health we're talking about!

What if I need to see a specialist or a surgeon? How do I choose one?

Sometimes your primary care physician doesn't have the necessary knowledge, expertise, or background to deal with a problem you have. The more complicated a problem, the more likely you will need to see a specialist to help treat it.

Generally, a specialist is far more experienced in performing certain procedures in the specialty (hence the word "specialist"). She knows what tests to order and what tests are a waste of money.

With some insurance companies, you can see a specialist who is in the network without getting a referral (this is usually true of PPOs). In other cases, you will need a referral from your primary care physician (this is likely with an HMO). But sometimes you may wish to see a specialist who isn't in the network.

For example, if you have Crohn's disease, and know a gastroenterologist who specializes in the disease but isn't in your plan's network, it's worth calling your insurer to find out what the rules are about using an out-of-network provider. Ask if you can get that provider covered at the in-network rate. In most cases, insurers would rather strike a deal up front than go through an expensive appeals process (which might be your next step). Be sure you get everything in writing as soon as a deal is made.

If you are looking for a specialist or a surgeon, the best place to begin your search is to ask your primary care doctor. To start with, your doctor knows you and your situation. Since most doctors are aware of the accomplishments of super-specialists who practice at large university hospitals or research-based facilities, your doctor can help you identify such experts. If you're having surgery, talk with people who have undergone surgery with the surgeon. One good way of finding the ideal surgeon is to find out who doctors go to when they need surgery for themselves or their families. The greatest compliment to a surgeon is paid when a doctor chooses to have him or her perform surgery.

If you can find a book or article relating to your problem, then the author (if he or she is a doctor) is likely to be a good choice. The other option is to find the name of a doctor or the head of a clinic or department who is actively publishing their medical research in this field. This doctor (or the head of the clinic) is likely to be an authority in the subject, and will be well informed of the latest advances in the field.

Once you have the names of specialists or surgeons who may be able to help you, you can follow the procedure for choosing a doctor described earlier in this section.

The doctor I chose isn't meeting my needs. How do I change doctors?

Changing doctors is never easy, because over time you build up a personal relationship with your doctor. However, you should consider changing doctors if you strongly feel that:

- *The doctor is incompetent.* He or she has ignored obvious symptoms, missed a diagnosis, prescribed the wrong drug, or can't get to the bottom of your problem.
- *The doctor does not communicate with you effectively.* Explanations are short and not easily understood, and you're not given time to ask questions. The doctor does not pay attention to your needs and concerns.
- *You have lost confidence in the doctor's skill and ability.*
- *You find the doctor is too inconsiderate.* He or she consistently makes you wait a long time for an appointment, fails to return your phone calls, or doesn't provide clinic time during evening or weekend hours.
- *Your doctor is too expensive.*

In the final analysis, remember that the most reliable test for a doctor's suitability for you is your own gut instinct—if you don't feel comfortable with your doctor, you shouldn't have him or her as your physician. On the other hand, if you have faith in your doctor's abilities and can trust that he or she will do the best for you, you are likely to get excellent medical care!

If your doctor is not right for you, then you will have to go through the process of researching other doctors. Make sure you think about what you don't like about your current doctor to make sure you don't duplicate the mistake. You don't have to make a big deal of notifying your current doctor that you're leaving. In fact, you don't have to notify your current doctor at all (although you may need to notify your insurance company that you're changing your primary care provider); your new doctor can request any medical records that are needed. (Also, a good habit to get into is to regularly ask for your doctor to send you copies of your records and test results so that you can have them on hand should you need to change doctors, see a specialist, or ask for a second opinion.)

Sometimes you like your doctor, but other circumstances mean you have to consider changing. For example, your doctor may decide to no longer accept your insurance. Often, more established doctors can be very selective about the health insurance they accept and will stop working with those who put too many constraints on their reimbursement. You may find that these constraints are affecting your doctor's ability to address your healthcare needs. In this case, you need to decide if you should find another health insurance plan, rather than changing doctors. This is where your partnership with your doctor may come into play.

If your doctor suddenly drops your insurance, make sure you find out why (you can ask the staff if you don't want to ask the doctor directly). You may find that your insurance policy has changed so dramatically that it may be worth the investment of purchasing a new policy. Have a candid conversation with someone who deals with health insurance on a daily basis, such as the billing manager. Ask what insurance she or he would recommend and why. You may uncover some details that will affect you in the future if they have not already impacted your bottom line.

If the reason you're changing doctors is your doctor is retiring, ask him or her to recommend a physician who accepts your insurance. Ask your retiring doctor to review your chart with the recommended doctor. Be sure the retiring doctor has a close enough relationship with the recommended physician so he or she could still have say in your treatment, if necessary. If the recommended doctor has time, it may be wise to set up an appointment with both doctors. Again, if your gut is uncomfortable with the recommended doctor, chances are your instincts are right.

Do not get in the habit of switching doctors, though. Your initial visit will cost about three times more than your following visits. Every time you have an initial visit, you will pay that initial fee. The visit will be more time-consuming, and you will be required to fill out paperwork.

Best advice: When you find a doctor you like, stick with him or her and build upon that relationship. It will save you a lot of time, money, and headaches. Just be sure you invest time in the initial background research of your doctor. You'll be glad you did!

How do I choose the right facility for a surgery or other treatment?

Use the Joint Commission, a nonprofit organization that accredits more than 20,000 healthcare organizations in the United States. Accreditation by the Joint Commission means that a healthcare organization (such as a hospital) has achieved a specific standard of patient care. Details about what that means can be found here: *www.quality check.org/consumer/searchQCR.aspx.*

Any facility accredited by the Joint Commission is required to have a complaint resolution process, and to give each patient a copy of the Patient Bill of Rights. This will usually be provided by a hospital representative and contain the contact information for a Patient Advocate, the person you get in touch with if you have any problems with your treatment.

The Joint Commission doesn't deal with billing, insurance, or employment issues. It can't tell you if your care (or a loved one's care) was poor or if anything was done wrong, nor can it settle differences between you and the facility. Instead, the organization checks to be sure the facility reaches standard of care, and if it does, accredits it for three years. After three years, the Joint Commission goes back to the organization to make sure it still meets those standards.

What if the facility I chose doesn't meet those standards and they've been accredited by the Joint Commission?

If you feel the Joint Commission standards for care are not being met, you can contact the Joint Commission at *www.jointcommission.org/report_a_complaint.aspx*. They will investigate the matter. They can also tell you if the facility has other complaints similar to yours, if the JC has written to the facility about your concern, recently visited the facility, asked the facility to make improvements, or changed the facility's accreditation status.

You can ask for documentation of the investigation to be included on any appeals process you are going through with the facility or choose to remain anonymous. When filing a complaint, you will need to include the name and address of the facility you are complaining about, and express your concern in one or two pages as it applies to the Joint Commission's standards. Be sure you also include your name and address (or e-mail address) if you would like follow-up information sent to you.

If an organization that is accredited by the Joint Commission knows you are behind an investigation, they may be more willing to work with you to resolve a billing matter that is a result of a violation of one of their standards, such as an infection or bed sores acquired in a facility.

For more information on the process, you can call 1-800-994-6610, fax 630-792-5636, or send an e-mail to *complaint@jointcommission.org*.

GETTING THE BEST CARE FROM YOUR DOCTOR

I've found a doctor I like. Now what?

Once you have a doctor you like, schedule a visit with a purpose like an annual checkup or concerning a specific medical issue. Most doctors do not have the time to sit and chat, so be sure you are going in with a purpose.

During that first visit you will learn a lot about just how easy it is to talk with the doctor. You will also find out how well the doctor might meet your medical needs. Ask yourself, did the doctor:

- Give me a chance to ask questions?
- Really listen to my questions?
- Answer in terms I understood?
- Show respect for me?
- Ask me questions to help understand my condition better?
- Make me feel comfortable?
- Address the health problem(s) I came with?
- Ask me my preferences about different kinds of treatments?
- Spend enough time with me?
- Explain things in a way I understand, including diagnosis, procedures, treatment, and what I can expect in the future?
- Give valid reasons for any treatment plans or tests ordered?
- Seem up to date with the relevant information?
- Seem open to discussion about alternative systems?

Trust your own reactions when deciding whether this doctor is the right one for you. However, you also may want to give the relationship some time to develop. It takes more than one visit for you and your doctor to get to know each other.

The first visit went fine. What are some other things I can look for in future visits to make sure I'm getting the best care possible?

It's always wise to make sure you're getting what you need from your doctor, whether it's the first visit or the fiftieth. Here are some additional questions to consider. Does your doctor:

- Prescribe medication that you can afford, such as generics?
- Fit you in if you are really sick, despite a tight schedule?
- Refer you to various resources (e.g., handouts, books, journals, Internet) to clarify information?
- Refer you to an appropriate specialist when required?
- Refer you to other support services or self-help groups?
- Call when additional information or test results are obtained?
- Give adequate consultation time?
- Have hospital privileges at a respected medical institution?

Keep in mind that there are some common warning signs of a bad doctor. No one of these is necessarily a sign in and of itself, but if they all routinely happen, or many of them happen, then you may not be getting the best care possible:

- Doesn't value your time, and makes you wait interminably on a routine basis.
- Seems more interested in treating your reports than in treating you.
- Doesn't spend enough time with you or explain treatment to you.
- Seems to be busy and rushed all the time.
- Orders tests whether or not they are needed.
- Doesn't explain your options to you.
- Discourages questions or refuses to answer them.
- Promises too much.
- Makes remarks like "I'll look into my crystal ball" or "That's my secret" rather than being transparent about treatment and prognosis.
- Discourages second opinions.

If you have noticed any of these red flags, discuss your concerns with your doctor. If you are still not satisfied after the discussion, you should consider looking for another physician.

How do I make sure that any tests the doctor orders are really necessary?

Here is a general checklist of questions you should ask your doctor when a test is recommended:

- Why is the test being ordered?

- Is it because the doctor is pretty certain about a diagnosis but needs the test to confirm it? In this case, what is the danger (if any) in starting treatment without the test?
- Is it because the doctor is puzzled about the diagnosis and is trying to rule out as many possibilities as possible?
- How definitive is the test?
- Is the test the gold standard for making the diagnosis?
- Will it reveal for sure that a condition is present or not, or must it be repeated or followed by more sophisticated tests?
- What precisely will the doctor be looking for in the results of these tests?
- What does the doctor hope to learn from the tests?
- How accurate is the test?
- Is there any pain?
- What are the side effects?
- What are the risks? (Many common tests do not involve any risks at all. Invasive tests—those that entail introducing instruments, such as endoscopes, or chemicals, such as barium, into the body—generally involve some risks. These risks may include infection, allergic reaction, or injury to an internal organ. Sometimes, a test may lead to complications, which are more dangerous than the benefit to be derived from the test results. While this is usually not the case, you need to consider the risk-benefit ratio of all tests, especially expensive and invasive ones.)
- What is the risk of not having the test done, and what are the alternatives?
- How will the results of the test change the course of your treatment? (This is the single most important question you must ask. If the answer is that the test won't change the treatment, you may not need the test at all.)

I understand why the test is needed. How do I make sure to get the most accurate result?

You can help improve the accuracy of certain tests by taking simple steps beforehand. Otherwise the test may need to be retaken or the results may be skewed, meaning the doctor may misdiagnose you.

Ask your doctor if you need to take any precautions before the test. For example, before a Pap smear, avoid douching, wearing a tampon, or using birth control foams or jellies for five days before the test, and avoid sex for two days before the test. Often for tests that involve drawing blood, you'll need to abstain from food and drink for a while beforehand.

Other tests require special preparations, and you must ensure that they have been carried out to get reliable results. Certain x-rays, such as barium enemas and intravenous pyelograms, require a laxative before the x-ray. If you don't do the preparation properly, inadequate results may occur, which will require a repeat preparation, a repeat x-ray, and a repeat bill.

In the final analysis, remember that medical tests can be very helpful in pinpointing your problem, but they need to be administered wisely and well.

I've heard of doctors misusing diagnostic or treatment technology. Can you explain what that means and how I can avoid it?

Many times people undergo unnecessary testing because it makes financial sense for a doctor or hospital, but not because it makes sense for your diagnosis or treatment plan. You need to be aware of the following inappropriate uses of medical technology:

- *Excessive use of technology when it is not required.* A prime example is an ultrasound scanning during pregnancy. While no one will dispute the fact that ultrasound scanning can yield invaluable information, ultrasound scans intended only to provide pictures for the baby's first album are inappropriate and costly.
- *Unethical use of technology.* Although prenatal diagnosis (through the use of ultrasound scanning) has been a very important tool for reducing the risk of birth defects, it can be misused for fetal sex selection.
- *Use of technology not suitable for a particular patient.* An example of this is advising IVF (in vitro fertilization) for all infertile patients just because the equipment and expertise are available and the procedure is (technically) feasible. However, for most infertile patients, there are many simpler treatment options available, and these should be fully explored before considering IVF.
- *Misuse of technology by unqualified persons.* A common example is the use of lasers or endoscopic equipment for complicated surgery. A doctor isn't sufficiently expert in using this technology just because he or she attended a two-day workshop and acquired a certificate.
- *Use of technology as defensive medicine.* Some doctors administer tests because it keeps them from being sued, rather than because the test is of benefit to the patient.

Thus, the crucial question arises: What can you do to protect yourself from being a victim of medical technology misuse? The answer is to make sure you are well informed, so that you can judge the technology and its relevance to you.

The National Institutes of Health (NIH) produces consensus statements in which leading medical experts from all over the world are invited to discuss the pros and cons of all the technological options available for dealing with a particular medical problem. These statements essentially guide doctors as to the appropriate use of the latest technologies. By using the information gleaned from such statements, or obtained from other sources intelligently, in cooperation with your doctor, you will ensure that the medical technology is used appropriately to provide the best possible care for your problem.

When should I think about getting a second opinion?

Getting a second opinion has become a common practice among doctors, which is why family physicians will often send you to a specialist, and the specialist, in turn, may consult other specialists. If the process is misused, you may pay for it in the end, not just financially but also through the stress of continual medical testing, perhaps lost work days, and more.

However, if you have a close relationship with your doctor, he or she shouldn't have any trouble explaining why he or she thinks the second opinion is needed. For example, your condition may be better treated by someone more familiar with it. At other times, your doctor may not be able to confirm a diagnosis (such as through testing) and would like another doctor's input before deciding on the best course of treatment.

Of course, there may also be times when you are not sure your doctor's diagnosis and/or treatment plan is correct or suitable, and may want to explore your options. This may require visiting another doctor and getting their take on the situation.

If two different doctors happen to reach the same conclusion, at least you know you are on the right track! However, don't always assume that just because the opinions of both doctors are identical that the diagnosis and treatment plan are the right ones. For example, if you have angina and you consult a cardiac surgeon, there is a high likelihood that he will advise you to undergo bypass surgery. A second cardiac surgeon is also likely to recommend the same. Therefore, getting a second opinion from a nonsurgical specialist (in this case, a cardiologist) can be helpful in preventing unnecessary surgery and costs.

Unfortunately, some doctors tend to refer patients unnecessarily to other members of their fraternity. Also, doctors will often cross-refer patients to each other for personal financial gain. In hospitals, especially, specialist consultation is often automatic and mandatory. This process is inevitably overused, which causes the patient's bill to shoot up! Thus, a hospitalized patient should ask the family physician (who should act as your medical manager) to intervene if the number of specialists involved in the treatment seems excessive.

When seeking a second opinion, consulting a specialist, or using an anesthesiologist or radiologist, be aware that they don't always accept the same insurance as your primary care doctor. Call your doctor to get the names of the medical providers who will be involved in your treatment, and verify with your insurer that they are still in your network. Also, don't assume that because your physician may be covered by your insurance, that the hospital/facility he or she is performing a procedure at also accepts your insurance.

What are some specific situations for which I should think about getting a second opinion?

You should think about getting a second opinion when any of the following happen:

- Your doctor is recommending surgery. Keep in mind that about 80 percent of all surgery is elective (that is, performed on a nonemergency basis). Surgery is an expensive alternative, and other treatment plans may work as well or could be tried first.
- Your doctor has diagnosed a rare, potentially fatal, or disabling disease. The original diagnosis could be incorrect and may need to be revised. Or, even if it is correct, there may be new or experimental treatments available at an institution specializing in the treatment of such a disease.
- Your symptoms persist unrelieved, and the doctor can provide no satisfactory explanation for them.
- Your doctor doesn't clearly explain the risks and benefits of the proposed procedures. You have the right to know the details about the risks and the costs as well as the potential benefits of any procedure, test, or surgery. It is preferable to get the relevant details in writing, so that you can review them later. It can be hard to assimilate everything while sitting in the doctor's office.
- Your doctor is recommending a procedure or a treatment plan that seems unnecessarily complex or expensive or both. Some doctors are prone to making excessive use of technology and testing in borderline situations, either due

to insecurity or to protect themselves against malpractice litigation.

- You don't trust that the doctor has done or can do all that can reasonably be expected. In other words, you don't trust the doctor. A lack of trust is as valid a reason as any other for getting a second opinion (or even for choosing another doctor entirely).

Again, I cannot emphasize how important it is to find the right doctor for you from the beginning, but it is okay to get a second doctor who may better understand your medical issue. If you get to the point where you lack the confidence in your doctor (as described in the previous point), you may make the wrong decision in a desperate situation, thus costing you more in time, money, tests, and so on. Take your time to find a doctor you trust when you do not need one!

How do I find a doctor to consult for a second opinion?

If your doctor is on board with your getting a second opinion, then the first course of action is to ask for his or her recommendation. If you're getting a second opinion because you're not sure your doctor is on the right track, then you'll want to look at the information in the "Choosing a Doctor" section in this part to help you decide whom to see.

It may be difficult to get an unbiased opinion from a second doctor who is a member of the staff in the same hospital as your doctor. If at all possible, consult an independent doctor in another hospital for a second opinion. Most medical insurance policies that cover consultation fees will pay for this.

A great source of second opinions is doctors who practice in public teaching hospitals. The staff members there are basically academicians. Since they teach medical students and residents, they are usually well read and well informed. Moreover, since they do not have a financial stake in providing you with advice, their information is likely to be reliable and accurate. It is not uncommon to have to wait for a long time to see these doctors, but in the end, it is well worth the wait.

It is also possible to get a second opinion from a doctor who practices alternative medicine like homoeopathy. Such an opinion will provide a completely different perspective of looking at a problem, and you may prefer this alternative.

You should also keep in mind that there are other ways of getting a second opinion apart from going to another doctor—such as using the Internet. Depending on the medical issue, all you have to do is Google your concern these days and you will get a myriad of opinions on remedies or procedures. However, use discretion and judgment. In many cases, there may be a hidden agenda, such as a paid advertisement. You may also want to tap into resources such as the National Institute of Health at *www.nih.gov*, or to use information from a well respected institution like the Mayo Clinic (*www.mayoclinic.org*).

What if the second doctor wants to redo all the tests the first doctor did?

A sure sign that the second doctor is taking advantage of you (rather than genuinely offering a second opinion) is if he or she orders tests immediately, instead of examining you and listening to what you have to say. Listening works both ways: patient to doctor and doctor to patient.

However, keep in mind that it is not uncommon for a doctor to reorder a test. After having an extensive conversation with you about the problem, the second doctor may conclude the initial doctor might have missed something. If the reordered test is targeted to the problem mentioned, that is okay, but if you find that a doctor is reordering every test, even ones that do not seem to be related to the health problem, question him or her immediately. If you are not satisfied with the response, find another doctor.

I got my second opinion. It disagrees with my first. Now what?

If it happens that your second opinion disagrees with the first, it's definitely worthwhile to get a third doctor (preferably one who has no vested interest in the matter) to advise you. It would also be prudent to discuss the differences in the two opinions with the concerned doctors so that they can explain and justify the reasons for the discrepancies in their diagnoses or plan of treatment.

CHOOSING THE RIGHT HEALTHCARE TREATMENT

What are some general things to keep in mind when evaluating a doctor's suggested course of treatment?

The decision-making process is different for each patient and depends on individual situations and requirements. Some patients may opt for expensive, high-tech treatment, while others in the same situation may prefer to wait and watch.

Each one of us has a different personal decision-making style. It is for you to choose which style best fits your own needs for making medical decisions:

- You may prefer to make the final selection of your treatment after seriously considering your doctor's opinion.
- You may prefer that the doctor make the final decision with regards to which treatment should be administered after seriously considering your opinion. Although some people do it, I would never recommend letting your doctor make the choice without hearing from you about your wishes and preferences.
- You may prefer to make the final selection on your own about which treatment you will receive, considering input from a number of sources, including other doctors, alternative health-care providers, and research you've done on the Internet.

It is imperative that you find a doctor who respects and understands your personal decision-making style. The reason for this is that throughout your treatment, your options may change and so will your priorities.

Try to be as realistic and open-minded as possible. While the final outcome will always remain unknown at the time you make your decisions, if you take the time and the trouble about considering your choice, at least you will have the satisfaction of knowing that you tried your best!

My doctor has recommended a treatment plan. I don't know what questions to ask about the plan. How do I know if it's right for me?

Your first step is to find out what kinds of treatment are available. You'll often find that a variety of treatment options exist, for instance:

- Medical therapy, which may include medication
- Surgery
- Physiotherapy, such as occupational therapy to treat an injury
- Radiation therapy (for some cancers)
- Waiting and watching (also called "masterful inactivity")

Your doctor will be able to make several recommendations about treatment. A second opinion might help the doctor uncover other treatments he may not have thought of in the past or help him make a decision on the best treatment for you. However, there are a number of important questions that you should always ask your physician so that you can make the best choice for yourself. These questions can help you build up a reservoir of medical information to assist you in your decision-making process regarding a particular treatment:

- How much will this treatment improve my chances of getting well (in other words, what are the benefits?)
- How much risk is involved in this treatment and what kind of risk is it?
- How long will the treatment take?
- How much will the treatment cost?
- Does undertaking this treatment eliminate other options?
- Are there other options if this treatment fails?

Talk to your doctor when you're deciding on what treatment you wish to follow, but remember that the final decision is yours. You will have to ascertain how much money you can spend, how much physical and emotional stress you can bear, and how much risk you are capable of assuming.

On the basis of these decisions, you will design your own medical treatment plan, custom-made for yourself! Not only will this step help you maintain control over your life as you proceed with the treatment, but it will also help ensure that you get good-quality medical care.

What other factors should I consider when choosing a medical treatment plan?

The main factors that will influence your decision include:

- Your diagnosis (or lack of one)
- The quality and availability of medical care (is it feasible for you to undergo the treatment where you live, or would you have to commute to a facility that may be miles from home?)
- The success rate of the proposed treatment
- The level of technology required for the treatment (is it available in your area?)

Personal factors include:

- Your age
- The time commitment needed for treatment (is it feasible for you to commit to an extensive treatment if you also have small children at home and a full-time job?)
- Your feelings, both physical and emotional
- Your job and career priorities (how will they be affected by the treatment plan?)
- Your financial resources (if the treatment forces you into bankruptcy, it may not be worth it!)
- Any ethical and religious concerns (for example, if you're unwilling to use animal products, can the treatment be done without them?)
- Your family and friends' reactions (particularly for extensive treatments, you will need a support network to see you through)
- Other obligations and commitments
- Your willingness to change your lifestyle (if you won't make the changes needed for the treatment plan to work, it may be best not to bother)
- Whether your prefer an aggressive or low-key approach to treatment

What if I need more help when making a medical decision?

There are tools available to help you research your options and make your own decisions. You should be happy with your choice and comfortable that you have made the best decision for yourself.

One program that can help you is the Foundation for Informed Medical Decision Making (FIMDM) (*www.fimdm.org*). FIMDM has developed shared decision-making programs for common medical problems (such as breast cancer and hormone replacement therapy) that enable you to make up your own mind while learning about all the pros and cons of various treatments.

Don't forget to visit the library—online, that is. Next to an extensive and leisurely consultation with your doctor, or a friend who is a doctor, the Internet is the best place for you to do research. An online library that can answer a lot of your medical questions can be found at *www.healthlibrary.com*. Also, explore *www.webmd.com*.

If you're unfamiliar with a particular topic, a medical encyclopedia is probably the best choice for gathering information. For an excellent overview of nearly any medical condition, the ideal guides include:

- *The American Medical Association Encyclopedia of Medicine* or *The British Medical Association Complete Family Health Guide*
- A reliable medical dictionary, such as the *Mosby Medical Encyclopedia* or Merriam-Webster's *Medical Desk Dictionary*
- *The Merck Manual* (home edition) is a superb compendium of almost every known disorder and describes causes,

symptoms, laboratory tests, diagnosis, treatment, and prognosis

If you are looking for information on a specific topic, you can use one of the Internet's search engines, such as Google. Simply type in the terms ("keywords") you're looking for. The search engine will point you to the relevant information you need. (A warning for novices: you may also be inundated by a flood of garbage, so you will need to carefully sift through what you find.)

There are many useful websites that provide consumer health information. For example, at *www.healthfinder.gov* you'll find health topics from A to Z, a directory of services, and other useful links. The great thing about locating a useful site is that it will often have a wide range of links, which will, in turn, point you to other helpful documents.

You can network with people all over the world to learn more about your treatment options. For example, electronic mailing lists exist for many diseases (Cancer-L deals with cancer). You can also send out e-mails to leading medical clinics and medical specialists from all over the world, and many will be happy to reply to you— free! There are also special-interest groups established on social media such as on Facebook, so that you can "talk" to thousands of people from all over the globe, who may be facing similar problems and looking for solutions. No matter what your final decision on your treatment is, be sure you are confident that it is the best course of treatment for you.

OBTAINING THE BEST PREVENTATIVE CARE

I know my insurance plan allows for some preventative care. How do I know what the best preventative care is?

As basic as it sounds, one of the most effective ways to lower your medical expenses over time is by preventing illness before it starts. To maintain a healthy lifestyle and incorporate preventative health measures, you can:

- Take advantage of wellness programs (many insurance companies offer these)
- Maintain a healthy weight
- Exercise regularly
- Kick unhealthy habits such as smoking (this may also lower your insurance premium)
- Have regular checkups

Which tests should be performed during a routine checkup?

Today, more patients see their doctors for checkups than for any other reason. While most patients assume that this is a standardized routine, a debate still rages in the medical profession regarding what tests should be performed, on whom, when, and how often.

Patients seem to fall into two extreme categories: those who get no routine medical care and those who receive excess medical care (screening tests), even though they do not really need it. Periodic tests and examinations should not become routine or part of a standard one-size-fits-all package. In order to be really effective, they need to be tailored according to a person's age, sex, family history, and personal risk factors.

Routine tests, such as electrocardiograms, chest x-rays, and full blood screening, have been found to provide little overall benefit for the healthy individual. If such is the truth, one may ask, "Why have these health checkup schemes have become so popular?" The answer is simple: They bring in the money! After all, hospitals and clinics can rake in much more money by screening droves of healthy people than by just treating sick patients.

There is the additional lucrative bonus that the screening tests will pick up abnormalities, which can convert a formerly healthy person into a patient who needs medical attention. However, when a screening test picks up a disease process early on, it is much easier to treat and cure than in the later stages of the disease. For example, benign colon polyps become cancerous over time if not removed and can be spotted via colonoscopy screening.

The major drawback of the tests conducted at present is that they are not very accurate. A large number of false positives crop up; that is, the test indicates that a patient has a disease when in reality she or he does not. Not only does an abnormal test result create a lot of anxiety and stress, it also leads to a merry-go-round of further tests and consultations in order to determine whether or not the original result has any significance.

The only routine tests that the U.S. Preventive Services Task Force recommends are:

- Periodic checkups for blood pressure for all adults. (High blood pressure is a leading risk factor for coronary heart disease, stroke, renal disease, and heart attack.)
- Total blood cholesterol measurement for men between the ages of thirty-five and sixty-five and women forty-five to sixty-five. (High cholesterol constitutes a risk factor for heart disease.) The frequency of testing is, however, not specified.
- Screening for colorectal cancer for individuals over fifty, by testing the stools for the presence of blood, or through sigmoidoscopy or colonoscopy. Colorectal cancer is common in the United States.
- Mammogram, an x-ray to detect the early signs of breast cancer, for women between fifty and sixty-nine, every one or two years.
- The Pap smear test to screen for cervical cancer, for sexually active women once every three years.
- Vision tests for children (before entering school) and for the elderly.
- Tests for elderly people (or those with specific complaints) to assess hearing loss.
- Routine blood tests such as sugar testing (to screen for diabetes), thyroid hormones tests (to screen for thyroid disease), and bone density tests for menopausal women (to screen for osteoporosis).

This task force refused to recommend widespread screening against other diseases for two reasons: either the tests had been found to have no merit, or there was not enough evidence to prove their benefit (that is, they did not help to improve either life expectancy or the quality of life).

In fact, screening tests could have a major negative impact on your health, which is why they should be undertaken with a great deal of discretion and caution. A good example of a screening test with potentially deleterious effects is genetic testing for the presence of certain cancer genes. Just because you have the gene doesn't always mean you will express the disease, but you will certainly become concerned and depressed worrying about the possibility.

Are there specific tests I should question before agreeing to take them?

Yes, there are several tests you should be wary of taking if your doctor orders them just as a matter of routine:

- *Chest x-ray.* A chest x-ray is not recommended as part of your periodic medical examination unless you have signs, symptoms, or a change of status in a chronic condition. If your primary care physician feels you are exhibiting any of these signs, ask what they are. Be sure that a board-certified radiologist is interpreting and performing the study, because they are the only people qualified to do this. In the end, ask for a copy of the report to be sent home so you and your primary care doctor can review the results.
- *Spirometry.* Unless you are suffering from significant shortness of breath, prolonged cough, or wheezing, your primary care physician should not recommend this test. Again, the preference is to have a board-certified pulmonologist perform the test rather than an internist. The internist may be able to handle the standard spirometry test, but not the more sophisticated one that involves a study of long diffusion.

- *Complete blood workup.* If you do not have a history of blood disease, cholesterol problems, etc., a whole workup is not necessary, but a fasting cholesterol test should be done every once in a while after the age of twenty. Be especially wary if your physician has a private lab in his or her office—it may not be covered by your insurance and may be serviced by the receptionist in the doctor's office rather than a full-time lab technician. Thus, more false positives may occur, which would lead to more money out of your pocket from multiple visits and an incorrect reading. If the doctor sends you to an independent lab, be sure your insurance accepts the lab.

- *Sigmoidoscopy versus colonoscopy.* The American Cancer Society used to recommend periodic flexible sigmoidoscopies in all patients over the age of fifty for colorectal cancer screening. Now, a complete colonoscopy is recommended for patients over the age of fifty because of the rise in cancer beyond the reach of the shorter sigmoidoscope. In addition, 30 percent of all patients over fifty will have benign, precancerous polyps at colonoscopy, which the gastroenterologist will routinely remove at the time of the procedure. Patients will be then instructed to return every three to five years for a follow-up colonoscopy to ensure the polyp(s) have not returned. Less experienced doctors may not have the training or ability to remove the polyps and may require you to have a second costly procedure with the specialist. It is wise then to take time choosing which doctor to perform your colonoscopy. Due to the complexity and high risk of perforation by an untrained internist or generalist, colonoscopies should only be performed by a board-certified gastroenterologist.

- *Electrocardiogram (ECG or EKG).* Everyone who is forty years and older who has a personal or family history of cardiovascular problems and anyone who is suspected to have cardiovascular problems should have a baseline EKG, but otherwise it is probably an unnecessary test. Of course, if you have a cardiac disease, it makes sense for an EKG to be part of a routine exam.

- *Stress test.* Anyone who is at risk for heart disease or even mild hypertension should probably have a stress test, but be sure it's performed by a board-certified cardiologist. If you get a stress test done by someone who is not very experienced or who is not familiar with the guidelines, you might get a false positive. A false positive might lead to a more complicated stress test, which is more costly and may be a risk for someone that actually has a complication.

- *Sonogram.* There may be many relevant reasons to undergo a sonogram (also called an ultrasound) but be sure that the results are interpreted by the right person. Who that right person is depends on what the ultrasound is for. A specialist knows exactly what they are looking for, and in the end, it will cost you less because his or her experience is in this area.

What else should I know about routine tests?

It is worth remembering that even the experts differ in their recommendations. For example, a major controversy is presently raging as to whether mammograms should begin at age forty or fifty. The rate of false positive results has been higher among younger women, possibly because women between the ages of forty and fifty have denser breasts than those over fifty. Recent studies show that young women stand a 50 percent chance of obtaining a false positive result from ten years' worth of annual mammograms. Some women endure intense anxiety and sometimes disfiguring biopsies before learning that they don't have cancer after all. In order to avoid this, it is important that you know your medical history and your family's history (siblings, parents, grandparents, and even your great grandparents). If you learn what is present in your family's health history, you can eliminate some unnecessary preventative screenings.

Another controversy relates to the need to screen a prospective candidate for prostate cancer, either by rectal examination or through a blood test for determining the presence of PSA (prostate-specific antigen). The PSA test measures the level of a specific protein in the blood that can indicate cancer and other prostate abnormalities. The drawback with this test, as with most screening tests, is that an elevated level of PSA is not indicative of prostate cancer. In fact, a number of patients who are normal will be found to have elevated PSA levels. In order to prove that they are not suffering from prostate cancer, they will be subjected to a prostate biopsy and sometimes even surgery to remove the prostate altogether.

The adverse consequences of widespread screening include:

- A large number of false positive results, causing needless anxiety and concern
- Unnecessary biopsies
- Harmful effects from aggressive treatments, including those for slow-growing cancers that may never have caused symptoms in a patient's lifetime and could have been left alone

As for testing for the early detection of other hidden cancers and early heart disease, the Task Force believes that physicians' time could be put to more productive use by discussing unhealthy behavior patterns with patients. After all, a doctor can do far more good for his patient by getting him to stop smoking than by subjecting him to a battery of tests or prescribing a motley bunch of pills for him.

How can I be sure to get the best benefit from a routine checkup?

Remember that you do not need to go in for a checkup every year. Individuals in their twenties and thirties who have no symptoms can safely undergo a physical once every two to five years. When you go for your periodic checkup, take all relevant medical records, your medical and family history, and all the medications you are taking (or have taken recently). Also, spell out clearly (to the doctor) the details about your lifestyle. Your doctor should talk to you and listen to you during your checkup—disease prevention is as important as detection.

People without any indicative symptoms do not need a chest x-ray, electrocardiogram, or complete blood work, since these do not provide the doctor with any clinically useful information. Therefore, you do not have to subject yourself to the delights of such tests just because they are offered as part of the package! Many patients naively believe that the more tests, the better the outcome. They're under the impression that obtaining more results means they're getting "better value for money."

However, such a belief is not true. A cost-effective checkup can be very simple, and should include the following: a physical examination, measuring height, weight, pulse, and blood pressure; blood tests for cholesterol; and screening for colorectal cancer. For women, in addition to these tests, the physical should include a Pap smear test and screening for breast cancer.

I know how to get the best care during routine situations. How can I be sure to get the care I need when my situation is urgent?

Use the emergency room for emergencies only—that's the most important step you can take in making sure you're not stuck with a huge bill that your insurance won't cover. Some of the most expensive medical treatments happen in the emergency room (ER), which is why it's better to get treatment elsewhere if you can. For example, if you're not feeling well, your doctor may be able to fit you in if you explain that your situation is urgent. Or you can visit an urgent-care facility rather than an emergency room. For example, if you cut yourself deeply enough to need stitches, but the injury isn't life-threatening, an urgent-care facility will be able to treat you at far less expense than an emergency room.

How can I tell the difference between something for which I should go to the emergency room and something that can be treated at an urgent-care facility?

Emergency care is usually defined as being necessary when a patient is suffering from, or could be suffering from, a life-threatening medical condition such as a stroke (sudden numbness in arms or legs) or a heart attack (chest pain). Other times to use the emergency room include:

- If you're experiencing severe shortness of breath or wheezing
- If you've injured yourself and the bleeding won't stop, even after you've applied pressure for ten minutes or so
- If you've suffered any type of head injury (even without bleeding)
- If you're throwing up blood or coughing it up
- If you suspect poisoning (either from something you ate or from something toxic to which you've been exposed)
- If you have bones broken in multiple places (or multiple bones are broken) or the break is particularly complicated (such as the bone has pierced the skin)
- If you're having an extremely unstable emotional episode, such as feeling suicidal or homicidal

Urgent-care centers can handle medical problems that need immediate attention but that aren't life threatening. Call your local urgent-care center ahead of time to get a better sense of what they can treat. This step will help you save money in the long run. Usually an urgent-care center can treat the types of things your doctor can treat but for which your doctor may not be available (for example, on the weekend or late at night), such as colds and flus, allergic reactions (if this is life threatening, bypass the urgent-care center and go directly to the ER), minor injuries (such as cuts and bruises), and simple fractures.

In addition, many urgent-care centers accept various types of health insurance and are more willing to negotiate prices for procedures, especially if you are unable to pay. Some urgent-care facilities even have a relationship with imaging centers nearby where they can help you get the best price on any radiology tests you need.

CONCIERGE HEALTHCARE

I've heard about concierge healthcare. Can you explain what this is?

Concierge healthcare is, essentially, private healthcare that depends less on public systems than traditional healthcare, and provides a higher level of service from your primary care provider. It also goes by names such as retainer medicine, cash-only practice, and direct care.

A primary care physician who provides concierge medicine may not take any insurance at all, and expects you to pay for all of his or her services out of pocket. Many of these providers promise availability to you for a monthly (or annual) fee (called a retainer) and offer quick callbacks and a higher level of personal attention than a traditional provider can offer. They are able to do this because they limit patient loads. Not accepting insurance and requiring a retainer allows them to reduce the number of patients they need to see in order to make a reasonable profit.

If you need treatment in a healthcare facility, concierge providers may be able to help you negotiate private payment to the facility (or you can use your health insurance to access that care).

Some advantages include being able to see the doctor without having to wait several days (or several weeks) for an appointment, and not being kept waiting for hours in the waiting room. Many concierge healthcare providers will give advice based on a telephone or Skype consultation (once they know you and your medical history). Some even make house calls! Unlike physicians in regular practice, they don't have to see you in the office in order to get paid.

There is some evidence that patients using concierge healthcare are more compliant with the doctor's orders and follow treatment plans more carefully.

There are a number of different business models currently in use, some of which are hybrids that accept insurance but charge you for extra services insurance won't cover (but which you may want, such as same-day appointments and immediate callbacks). Be sure you understand what your concierge provider is offering before agreeing to it.

What types of doctors offer concierge healthcare?

Most are primary care physicians in general practice, such as internal medicine specialists or family practice doctors. Pediatricians are also a core group offering this service, and other providers, such as dentists, are now offering concierge healthcare.

Does concierge healthcare really mean I get more personal attention?

As with anything, your results may vary, but most concierge primary care physicians report caring for far fewer patients than those in a regular practice. Most say they see no more than six or eight patients a day. Contrast that to a physician in a regular practice who might see three or four times that many patients. A concierge physician might have three or four hundred patients total in his or her practice, while a physician in regular practice might have ten times as many.

How can concierge medicine save me time and effort?

Many healthcare concierge services offer a telemedicine component where you can talk to a doctor without exposing yourself to other people who might be sick (and save yourself a trip to the doctor's office). One such example is *Connect2docs.com*, where a small monthly fee gives you access to a contracted, board-certified physician at any time.

Most of these telemedicine services have HIPAA-compliant webcams with a guarantee that you'll hear from a physician within a certain amount of time, as well as transcription services that allow you to download your conversation. In addition, some providers will even offer extra services such as a once-per-year check on certain bloodwork at no extra cost, as well as pharmacy savings and help on negotiating some of your medical bills.

I bet it's pricey. How much can I expect to spend on the annual retainer?

The answer is "it depends." You may be able to find a low-cost provider who charges a retainer of as little as a few hundred dollars per year, or you may spend many thousands. Many healthcare concierge physicians are trying to find ways to make healthcare more affordable and so they keep their retainer costs low, while others are focused on providing VIP services (and catering to a high-end clientele), meaning they charge significantly more. If you're not aiming for VIP services, you can probably expect to spend two or three thousand dollars a year for the physician's retainer.

Most people who use concierge healthcare pay for it in addition to their traditional health insurance coverage (note that concierge healthcare does not work well with HMOs since HMOs require an in-network primary care physician to serve as the clearinghouse for all referrals). Some concierge physicians are able to offer services to those on Medicaid.

You may be able to pay for the retainer with funds from your HSA or FSA.

What if I need an EKG and some blood work? Will I have to pay for that out of pocket?

Most concierge providers cover basic care and routine testing in the retainer fee, so usually you won't have to pay extra for things such as an EKG or a blood glucose test. For testing and procedures that go beyond the routine, most concierge physicians have a clear menu of pricing and they will tell you exactly how much a procedure or test will cost before you have it done. For example, an ultrasound may cost $100 to $250. A strep test might cost $15. Most will expect full payment at the time of service.

Many concierge practices will coordinate with you to use your insurance benefits at facilities that provide the needed testing and procedures.

Some may also be able to provide for discounted medications through arrangements with local pharmacies.

What if I get sick while I'm away from home?

Your concierge physician may be able to arrange a phone or Skype consultation with you if you become ill while traveling. Members of MDVIP (*www.mdvip.com*) can see any doctor who is also a member of MDVIP, meaning that you may be able to consult with a physician who has access to all of your medical records even if you're away from home.

Some high-level concierge services will offer medical escorts and other premium care for individuals who become ill while traveling.

Sounds great! Where do I sign up?

At present, it's estimated that only about 6,000 physicians in the United States are offering some type of concierge healthcare. However, more and more providers are adopting the model. You can find out if a doctor in your area is offering this model of healthcare by checking the American Academy of Private Physicians, *www.private physicians.com/#*. MDVIP is a network of concierge physicians. Find out more about them at *www.mdvip.com*.

PART 4

CONTROLLING YOUR HEALTHCARE COSTS

Having a good insurance plan helps reduce your out-of-pocket expenses, but you'll find that it's easy to make a mistake that ends up costing you plenty, such as accidentally using an out-of-network provider or thinking a procedure is covered when it isn't.

In this part, we'll talk about how to avoid those costly mistakes (and what to do if you can't avoid them). We'll also talk about what you need to know about your medical records and how that relates to billing, how to read a medical bill, and what types of incorrect billing are most common (and how to spot them).

We'll also talk about how to control costs for everything from that root canal to sessions with a mental health therapist. If you're worried about how to pay for an upcoming procedure, we've got you covered: you'll find out all the many different ways you can keep a lid on expenses, from negotiating ahead of time to taking advantage of a hospital's charitable program.

Finally, we'll give some pointers on how to use preventative medicine to improve and maintain your health—and help control your healthcare costs by reducing the likelihood of your needing expensive medical care.

HOW TO DEAL WITH INSURANCE PROBLEMS

How do I deal with a denied claim?

Dealing with a denied claim can seem like the biggest waste of time, but if it will potentially save you a lot of money, it is worth the extra few hours of effort needed to get that denial turned around.

Unfortunately, many people don't know where to start and give up too fast. Many times, this is what the health insurer is counting on, but if you can prove that you are organized, understand your rights, and are not willing to back down, they may be the ones to give in. Many times it is not until you enter the third denial process that your health insurance company will finally accept your claim.

If a claim is denied, don't delay. You'll need to respond quickly in order to preserve your rights. Start by reading your benefit package. It may be that simple and the answers you seek may be obvious.

If that's not the case, then request an explanation in writing as to why your claim was denied. Call and ask to talk to someone if you still do not understand, especially if your benefits package is unclear. If you're still not satisfied with the answer, ask to speak with a supervisor. You may find that the claim was coded incorrectly or the wrong information was submitted. In that case, it may be a simple fix, but if it is not, you may have to take it a step further and file an appeal.

How do I file an appeal?

The appeal process varies depending on your state and the insurance company, but in general you will need to follow these steps. First, you will need to put your appeal in writing. Check the insurance company's website or plan information to find out what needs to be included with the appeal. Be sure you include all pertinent information. It is always helpful to include the following:

- Your appeal letter
- A letter from your doctor and specialist addressing the specifics of your case
- Any pertinent information from your medical records
- Any articles from peer-reviewed clinical journals that support your case

Be sure to document everything, including the times you called the insurance company, the names of representatives you spoke with, and what they said. Include this information in your appeals letter.

Make several copies of the letter and other documents such as itemized bills you may need to include, and keep a copy for your records. Send your letter and the supporting documentation via U.S. mail (be sure to verify where to send all of the materials) to the insurance company.

After you send everything to the appropriate parties with time stamps, be sure you follow up with a phone call, e-mail, and even fax. Check your benefits package and verify your time limits because if you wait too long, your claim may be denied based on it being out of the claim period.

You may also want to send copies of your appeal letter to your state representative, your state's department of insurance, your state's health department, and your state's office of consumer affairs (usually part of your state's attorney general's office).

The key is to document and keep accurate records of whom you spoke to and what they advised you to do. Do not give up until you get an answer you can accept. If the rule you are debating was written in your policy and your health insurance is unwilling to work with you on a viable solution, you may just want to take notes and switch plans during your next open enrollment period.

What do I do if a procedure I need is not fully covered by my insurance?

It is not uncommon to realize at the last minute that a procedure is not covered or not fully covered. If you have time, contact your doctor and ask if there is an alternative procedure that might be covered by your health insurance.

If you have determined that you need a procedure that is not covered by your insurance, consider asking your physician for a discount. Many physicians, if they know your situation, are more than willing to accept a cash rate up front for a fraction of the total cost. In addition, be sure to inquire if you can have the procedure performed at an outpatient surgical center as opposed to a hospital. Many times, surgical centers are a lot cheaper, because you don't have the overhead.

If you must have your procedure done at a hospital, be sure to call around and compare prices. Depending on your procedure and the hospital, you may be able to request an estimate in writing and a discount up front. You can actually do this more easily with an outpatient surgical center. However, smaller hospitals are more than willing to cut a deal when they know other facilities that are comparable may get your business.

Another option is checking into patient assistance programs such as a charity care. Charity cares are programs that are set up to provide those who need financial assistance with hospital care. Depending on the type of program and if the hospital is set up as a nonprofit, the institution may have been allotted certain tax breaks conditional on donating a percentage of services to those who may need it but are unable to pay. Even if you already have had a procedure that you find your health insurance has not covered, you may find that you may qualify for some of these discounts.

In addition, remember that many hospitals also outsource some of their services, such as radiology, anesthesiology, laboratories, and pharmacies. Try to learn ahead of time what types of services may be outsourced before getting your procedure done, so you can contact these providers directly and negotiate a flat rate ahead of time. In fact, if there are any diagnostics (labs, MRIs, or x-rays) that need to be done prior to your procedure and are not covered by your health insurance, try pricing imaging centers and laboratories outside the hospital and using one of those instead of the likely more expensive hospital. Make sure your doctor is aware you're doing this. She or he may have contacts who can help you get a better deal.

Bottom line: You should try to find out what is covered and what is not *before* undergoing a procedure. If your procedure is not covered by your insurance, determine what is needed during the procedure, including medication that you may be able to bring in from home, as well as your own facial tissue and slippers!

UNDERSTANDING BILLING AND RECORDS

What does my medical record have to do with my medical bills?

As soon as you make that initial appointment for the doctor/clinic/hospital, a medical record is created, and it is from that medical record the billing is made.

Medical records can be voluminous documents and they can be difficult for the nonclinician to understand. They include physician's notes, reports, forms, x-rays, and charts, sometimes in no specific order. If you review your record, you can comprehend the details of your billing a little more easily. Remember, though, just because you don't recognize the charge doesn't mean the procedure associated with it wasn't done. So save yourself some embarrassment and review your record (and the billing) with a professional before pursuing a complaint.

How do I get copies of my medical records?

Simple! Just ask your doctor or hospital and sign a records release form. Remember that you have a legal right to your medical records, though technically the documents belong to the healthcare provider who generated them. In most cases, the information about you belongs to you. Your healthcare provider (whether a doctor, hospital, or something else) may charge you for making copies, and you will need to pay the required amount. Most will be happy to estimate this cost for you ahead of time.

You should read your records because you are being charged, you have a right to know what procedures/treatments are being performed and why, and you should verify that what you're being told is what is being written in the medical record. Some nurses and doctors still don't know that patients have the right to see their own medical records, so you need to be aware of your rights.

Some consumer advocates argue that it is a good idea for patients in a hospital to take a look at their own medical charts routinely, to make sure that the doctors and nurses have written down everything accurately. After all, medical notes can be inaccurate or incomplete, leading to confusion about your care, either now or in the future.

When you receive the bills, check to make sure they accurately reflect the procedures you have undergone and take into account any applicable insurance coverage you may have. Some errors, such as wrong codes, are common, and you may be billed for healthcare you never received. Codes are used as a shorthand method of describing your diagnosis and what was done to treat your symptoms. For example, the code "101" could mean "common cold." If you have other symptoms, another code is used to identify these complications. If someone makes a mistake and says you have "101," a cold, when in fact you have "110," which is the code for mild infective and parasitic disease, then your insurance company might deny a claim for certain tests because a common cold does not call for them.

Contact the appropriate billing offices if you think you've found a mistake. If you received an explanation of benefits from your insurance company that you believe is wrong, ask the company to review your claim.

What kinds of documents are in my medical record?

A variety of documents are found in most medical records. They may go by different names, but they include this type of information:

- The identification sheet is a form that originates at the time of admission. This form lists your name, contact information, name of emergency contact, and so on.
- History and physical/clinical findings is a document that describes factors such as:
    - Any major illnesses and surgeries you have had
    - Any significant family history of disease
    - Your health habits
    - Current medications you're taking
    - Your height, weight, blood pressure, pulse, respiration rate, any particular symptoms you may have described, and details of your physical examination.
- Progress notes are made by the doctors, nurses, and therapists caring for you; they reflect your response to treatment and medical professionals' observations and plans for continued treatment.
- Consultation notes contain the opinion about your condition made by a physician other than your primary care physician. Sometimes, a consultation is performed because your physician needs the advice and counsel of another physician. At other times, a consultation occurs when you yourself request a second opinion.
- Physician's orders record your doctor's directions regarding your medications, tests, diet, and treatments.

- Imaging and radiology reports describe x-ray results, mammograms, ultrasounds, or scans. The actual films are usually stored in the radiology or imaging departments (although with digital records becoming more and more common, the actual films can be accessed by any authorized person in the facility).
- Electrocardiogram (EKG) reports.
- Lab reports describe the results of tests conducted on blood, sputum, urine, and other body fluids. Common examples would include a urinalysis, complete blood count (CBC), cholesterol level, and throat culture.
- Authorization forms include signed consents for admission, treatment, and surgery.
- The operative report describes the surgery performed and gives the names of the surgeons and assistants involved.
- The anesthesia report documents the preoperative medication, anesthesia given, and the response to anesthesia during surgery.
- The pathology report describes tissue removed during an operation (if any) and gives a diagnosis based on the examination of that tissue.
- The graphic sheet is generally a graph used to plot your temperature, pulse, respiration, and blood pressure over a particular period of time.
- The discharge summary presents a concise account of your hospital stay, which includes the following information:
    - The reason for admission
    - The significant findings from tests
    - The procedures performed
    - The therapies provided
    - Your response to treatment
    - Your condition at discharge

- Instructions given to you about medications, activity, diet, and follow-up care.

If you understand what these various documents mean, you can understand how they're used in billing. So, for example, a radiology report will result in two different types of charges. One is the technical component—the actual taking of the x-ray, which requires the use of specialized equipment and a technician to perform the actual test. The other is the professional interpretation of the result of the x-ray, usually performed by a doctor (more specifically, a radiologist).

So when you get a medical bill and it says "pelvic x-ray," this is considered the technical component. This does not include the interpretation of the x-ray (for example, if the radiologist found a fracture). The interpretation of the x-ray will be charged on a separate bill known as the professional component. These bills might arrive in your mailbox months apart from each other, which is why it is important to get a summary of all procedures performed before leaving the facility. This way you can track what bills to expect.

What else do I need to know about medical records and my care—not to mention my finances?

Your medical records can prove extremely important in case you are unhappy with the care you received. If you need to complain about your doctor or hospital, the records can be used to support your claim, even for a discount in your bill. These days, most hospitals have patient advocacy groups that will try to resolve these issues before anyone has to get sued. Often times, if an unanticipated complication occurs in the course of your care, the hospital will gladly give a discount rather than face a potential malpractice claim.

The same holds true if you do not understand why something was done or not done. You have a right to ask for an explanation and should be given one you can understand. For example, due to the shortage of nursing staff, many hospitals will place Foley catheters in their elderly patients for the convenience of the staff (this way, nurses do not have to attend to the patient as much because if a patient needs to urinate, he or she just goes through a tube instead of calling the nurse for assistance). As a patient, you are being charged for the Foley catheter as well as the catheterization. If you are not satisfied with the explanation given by the nurse, be sure to ask a doctor before it becomes a procedure and equipment charge on your bill.

In addition, keep in mind that you are charged for every meal, even if you do not request it or missed it. So, if you feel the need to skip a meal, be sure the nurse documents that you requested no meal and be sure it does not show up on your bill months later. You will likely forget the details of the charges on your bill, so it is important to write it down and document your concerns to the hospital administration at the time of the hospitalization. The hospital medical bill can take months to arrive, long after your insurance has paid its part of the bill.

Your medical records also provide information to your insurance company when you need to claim reimbursement for expenses for medical treatment. If procedures/treatments are not being documented, or are not being documented appropriately, it may cost you more in the end.

Your medical records serve many purposes. They are:

- The basis for planning your care and treatment
- A way for health professionals to communicate about your care

- Basic data for health research and planning
- Verification of services and treatment covered by your insurance
- A legal document describing the care you received

Is there any one thing I should be on the lookout for when I review my medical records?

Pay particular attention to the diagnosis listed in your record. Be sure it corresponds with your treatment. For example, if the reason you are admitted is for chest pain, and in the course of testing it is discovered that you have iron deficiency anemia and require colonoscopy/upper endoscopy, make sure the anemia diagnosis is clearly outlined as urgent and the in-hospital evaluation necessary. Otherwise, your insurance company may deny the claim for the inpatient workup, and you may get stuck with the bill.

Most insurance companies have a protocol of treatments they expect the doctor to follow in order to get reimbursed. If the doctor prescribes a different treatment or set of tests that the insurance carrier is not used to seeing, it is likely you will not get reimbursed. This is why it is better to catch a problem before it becomes an issue by reviewing your record as soon as it becomes available. If such an error happens, your doctor should have an explanation and be able to write a letter on your behalf to your insurance company stating the reasons the treatment was necessary based on your diagnosis. That way, reimbursement should not be a problem.

I am being admitted to the hospital for treatment. What should I do that will help me lower the costs or at least understand what they will be?

If your hospitalization isn't for an emergency, meaning you have time, check your insurance policy to find out just what it will cover and how much it will pay. Be sure to carefully review the section on exceptions and exclusions. It will tell you what your plan will not cover. Here is a list of actions you should consider taking before you are admitted:

- Phone the hospital's billing department and ask them the daily rate of the room and what is included. Can you request a semiprivate room? (Having a roommate will lower your costs, and some insurance companies only cover the charge for a shared room, not a private room.)
- Assume everything is à la carte (from the facial tissue to the toothbrush), unless you were told otherwise. Make a list and ask what to bring in from home to reduce these charges. Be sure to document the person you spoke with, the price that was quoted, and what was included.
- Ask your doctor to estimate your cost of treatment. Also, ask if you can bring your regular prescriptions from home to avoid paying for medications administered at the hospital.
- Make sure that everyone who will be treating you—from the surgeon to the radiologist—participates in your insurance plan.
- Schedule the procedure as early as possible. By scheduling your procedure early in the morning, you may be able to avoid backups in the operating room (OR) that may cause you to

stay at the hospital longer than you otherwise would. Also, try to schedule your procedures early in the week, so if there is a backup in the OR, you're not forced to stay over the weekend when staff is limited, causing a delay in your discharge.

- Ask your doctor if you can have your lab work or other screenings such as an MRI, CT, or x-ray done at a separate facility that will charge less than the hospital does. Be sure you schedule these tests/screenings well in advance of your procedure to avoid any delays.
- Arrange a payment plan. For more expensive procedures, be sure the hospital does not charge you a large amount of interest. If that is the case, you might as well pay for the procedure on your credit card and gain frequent flyer miles in the process!

What should I do during my hospital stay to help keep track of expenses?

You can do a number of things to help ensure that you are billed correctly for your treatment.

- Keep your own log of tests, medications, and treatments. If you unable to do so, ask a friend or loved one to do it for you.
- It is fine to be inquisitive while you are in the medical facility; it is your right to get an explanation if you do not understand why something is done.
- Keep track of the doctors (and other healthcare providers) visiting you. Every doctor who examines you while you are

staying in the hospital will charge you. Even the doctor who pops his head in to ask how you are doing and orders some medications will charge you for the visit. This is why it is important to maintain a good relationship with your primary care physician/surgeon performing the procedure. If he or she agrees that no other physician needs to see you, be sure you're not charged for a consultation. If you do not want to be seen by any other doctor until you and your primary care doctor are able to talk, let the nurse know and be sure he or she documents that in your medical chart. If possible, your primary care doctor should let you know when a specialist or another physician is needed ahead of time.

Once I get my bill, what should I do?

You can do a few things to make sure that you're not overpaying for your treatment.

- Ask for an explanation. If there are items you don't understand on your bill, call the hospital's billing department and your insurer and ask them to explain.
- At some point, you will receive an explanation of benefits (EOB) from your insurance company (if you're on Medicare, you will receive a summary notice). It will say, "This is not a bill." Don't toss it in the trash (however much you're tempted to do so). Examine it. It will tell you how much the hospital is charging, what your insurance plan will cover, and what you will have to pay out of your own pocket in deductibles and copayments.

- When you get your bill, read it carefully. Compare your bill to the log/journal you made along with your explanation of benefits (EOB) and estimated costs you requested before you were admitted. Look for any discrepancies and bring them up with the appropriate billing departments.
- Always ask for an itemized bill, as well as your medical records to confirm whether or not you received the treatments and medications you've been billed for. Every state now requires hospitals to provide itemized bills.

Is there anything I *shouldn't* do when paying a medical bill?

Yes! There are several things you shouldn't do.

- Never pay your bill before leaving the hospital, even if you're told that it's required. In order to review a bill carefully, you will have to take it home and compare it with your insurance company's explanation of benefits. Be sure you ask for a complete itemized bill. Don't feel pressured no matter who tells you that you must pay the full bill before you are discharged. Don't make the payment even if it is just a small balance.
- Don't ignore your bill! As soon as a healthcare provider interacts with you, the billing process begins. However, depending on your health insurance, income status, medical expenses, and resources, your final bill may be negotiable. If your case involves a car accident or workers' compensation issue, and someone else will be responsible for the charges, you still need to be sure to pay close attention to the process.

- Don't assume someone else is taking care of the problem. Even if you have an attorney involved (for example,
  because you were injured in an accident), don't assume
  that your attorney will take care of everything. A bill that
  slips through the cracks and isn't paid lands on *your* credit
  report, not the attorney's.

In fact, most miscommunications and mistakes over medical billing happen when you have a representative involved. You should
always notify the billing department in writing that you have a representative (such as your attorney) involved, and verify with your representative what has and will be negotiated with all parties involved.

What happens if I just don't pay the medical bill?

More and more healthcare providers have hired collection attorneys
on a contingency basis to file judgments against people who do not
pay their bills. This will go on your credit history. Typically, you will
receive at least three statements from the facility before any action is
taken against you.

Do not depend on your attorney or representative to handle this
for you. Follow up and make sure something is in your file under your
medical record number with all parties that are involved with your
treatment.

In some situations, the medical facility will file a judgment against
you automatically because of lack of communication and not knowing
what is going on, so if you have acquired any assets you will not be
able to liquidate them until all outstanding medical bills are paid. On

the other hand, some medical facilities do not have the means to hire a collection attorney and will write off any unpaid bills as bad debt if no action has taken place in six months. It is likely, however, that this bad debt will be reported to credit agencies even if no further debt collection steps are taken.

How can I tell if my bill is accurate?

It can take a few days, weeks, or even up to a year for the healthcare facility to produce the itemized bill and records. By this time, you may have forgotten details of your hospital stay and may not recall what specifically should or should not appear your bill. That's why keeping a log of your treatment while you're in the hospital is so important. If, for example, the bill says you received an asthma treatment and you know you didn't, you can flag that as a problem to follow up on.

If more than a few weeks have gone by since treatment and you haven't received a bill, call the facility's billing department and ask when and from whom you should expect to receive these documents.

When you finally receive the itemized bill, pull out your calculator and add the charges up yourself. There may be discrepancies in the totals with the bill and an extra zero might have made its way in somewhere, seriously increasing the amount of the bill. Double check to make sure treatments and procedures weren't billed twice.

About 80 percent of all hospital bills contain errors. This can increase your tab by about 25 percent. Check your log against your medical file, which you can order in the hospital's billing office.

If you find an error, send a certified letter requesting a corrected bill. Explain the errors you have found. Don't let the hospital/

medical facility tell you that your insurance will take care of it. Send a copy of all documentation (including the letter outlining the error) to your insurer.

When the billing department responds (this may require you to follow up), be sure to get their answer in writing. If they call first, be sure to make a note of the person to whom you spoke and their contact information so you can follow up on it. Keep copies of everything. If the error is still unresolved by the date promised, send your complaint in writing with copies of all documents and correspondences to the office of consumer affairs at your state attorney general's office.

Billing discrepancies occur often, and can be challenged only if you have documented exactly what happened. This process can be painstaking and difficult, but it can save you thousands of dollars.

What are some common billing mistakes I should look out for?

There are a number of these:

- *Duplicate billing.* Always check your bills carefully and make sure you haven't been charged twice for the same service, supplies, or medications. Mistakes do happen, so if you notice them on the bill, call the insurance company and the hospital billing department immediately so both agencies can rectify the bill. Then put the information in writing and send a certified letter to the hospital (with a copy to the insurance company).

- *Services never rendered.* Did you get every service, treatment, and medication for which you are being billed? If you were in a semiprivate room, make sure you're not being charged for private room. Were you charged for a box of facial tissue or slippers you brought from home? Did you skip a meal and were you charged for it?
- *Operating room time.* It's not uncommon for hospitals to bill for more time than you actually use. Compare the charge with your anesthesiologist's records. Rates may vary from $500 to more than $2,000 per half hour of operating room time. If you compare your bill with the anesthesiologist's record (or with his/her separate bill for professional services), you may find that you were billed for five hours for a procedure that actually took only four.
- *Upcoding.* Hospitals sometimes charge for a higher-priced item when a lower-cost one was ordered or used. For example, the doctor may order a generic drug, but your bill lists the pricier brand name. Or your diagnostic code may reflect a more serious condition requiring more costly procedures. You can double check the doctor's orders against the diagnosis to make sure it is consistent with the procedures listed on your bill. If you do not know these codes, be sure to go over them with a billing manager.
- *Wrong diagnosis.* At the top of your itemized bill, you will see a code for the diagnosis on the basis of which you entered the hospital. Charges are based on this diagnosis. If this code is incorrect, your insurance company may deny your claim because your treatment may not have been the protocol for the diagnosis listed.
- *Keystroke error.* A computer operator accidentally hits the wrong key on a keyboard. It can cost you hundreds of dollars and result in an incorrect charge for a service you didn't get.

- *Canceled work.* Your physician ordered an expensive test and then canceled it, but you were charged anyway.

When I paid my bill, the clerk mentioned that I can take the expense off my taxes. What does that mean?

The IRS allows you to deduct unreimbursed medical bills that exceed 10 percent of your gross income. That's a high bar, but the list of eligible expenses is extensive, including insurance premiums, dental x-rays, fertility treatments, prescribed weight-loss and smoking cessation programs, as well as LASIK eye surgery.

A medical expense is generally defined as unreimbursed (that is, your insurance or some other organization didn't cover it) medical and dental expenses paid for the diagnosis and treatment of a disease. So you can't write off that nose job because it is purely cosmetic, but if there's a medical reason why you need reconstructive surgery on your nose, then that is a legitimate medical expense and can be written off (or at least the amount that exceeds 10 percent of your gross income can be written off).

For more information, visit *www.irs.gov/taxtopics/tc502.html.*

CONTROLLING MEDICATION COSTS

I need a medication for a chronic condition. What are some ways I can control my medication costs?

One basic way to save money is by ordering your prescriptions through the mail. If you belong to a prescription drug plan (through your health insurance), you may be able to get a three-month supply of your prescription drug through the mail for the same price you would pay for a one-month supply at your neighborhood pharmacy.

Another way to save is to ask your doctor to prescribe a less-expensive generic drug whenever possible (your pharmacist can recommend some options).

Here are some questions to ask that may help you control the cost of your medication:

- Does your insurance cover the type of prescriptions that you need? If not, perhaps you should switch plans or ask the company to add your drugs to their formulary (the list of medications for which they will provide reimbursement).
- Can your healthcare provider give you samples? This can be a good way to check whether a drug will work before you fill a prescription. (You can also have a prescription partially filled to make sure it works for you. If it doesn't, then you're not throwing away most of a bottle of medication.)

- Can your physician provide a drug voucher (instead of a sample)? The drug voucher is a coupon for the drug, which you would take to the pharmacy for free medication. The drug company later reimburses the pharmacy for the cost of the drug.
- Do you qualify for a pharmaceutical company's drug assistance program?
- Do you qualify for a state assistance program?
- Are over-the-counter drugs available that might give the same or similar results? For example, prenatal vitamins may be $20 for 100 tablets. These are covered by some insurance plans, with a $7 copay for thirty days' worth of pills. So ninety tablets would cost $21 using that insurance, but $20 for 100 tablets without insurance.
- Is one pharmacy less expensive than another pharmacy? You might be surprised at how costs vary. Call around to find out.
- Does your physician know how much the prescription should cost? If not, ask the office staff to call the local pharmacy while you are there to check prices. This is often a great eye opener for doctors. Cipro 500 mg (an antibiotic) can run more than $150 for a ten-day course. There are no generic substitutes, but your physician may be able to offer an alternative.

How can I make sure my insurance company will help me pay for my medication?

People who have an ongoing need for medication sometimes make the mistake of purchasing health insurance that does not have a drug plan or has a limited drug plan. Be sure to read the drug benefits under the insurance plan you choose or call the insurance plan and ask what medications they cover. You may even want to consult with your primary care physician as to which insurance companies have the most flexible drug plans.

Your insurance company will have a list of prescription drugs that they will cover, called a drug formulary. Usually, this means generic rather than brand-name drugs. The list may be subject to change. If you do not keep up with the list you may find that a drug you have been using is no longer covered—and often you find this out only when you go to the pharmacy to pick up the prescription.

If this happens, call your doctor right away. Often you can use a comparable drug that is covered.

A friend of mine says that she saves money by getting several months' worth of medication from her pharmacy at a time. How does that work?

Some insurances company may allow you more than a month's worth of medication at a time. There is a per-ticket fee for every prescription (to pay for the bottle, label, sack, paperwork), so getting several months' worth of medication at once can remove some of the per-ticket fees. That's how the price can be lower. If you have to make a copayment every time you get a prescription filled, then getting three months' worth of medication at one time saves you two copayments. This depends on your insurer though, so please don't blame the pharmacist if your insurer doesn't allow it. For controlled drugs, there is very little possibility that you can get more than one month's worth at a time. Please do not expect the pharmacist to break the law for you.

What can you tell me about using generics to control medication costs?

This may be one of the best cost-saving methods in healthcare! Generic drugs are the chemically equivalent, lower-cost version of a brand-name drug. The generic version of a drug usually becomes available when the brand-name drug's patent protection expires, or the FDA regulation and oversight is complete. In both cases, the cost is usually about half the price of the brand-name version.

All drugs have a generic name. When a pharmaceutical company first develops a new drug, it gives the drug a generic name or chemical name. The company then gives the drug a brand name as part of its marketing plan. Thus, generic drugs are just as regulated as brand-name drugs; essentially they are the same drug. The generic and brand-name drug have the same active ingredient, and there have never been reports of serious differences between them. For example, the generic name for Tylenol is acetaminophen. If you purchase generic acetaminophen in the same strength, it will do the same thing Tylenol does.

By federal law generics have the same amount of active ingredients as brand-name drugs. The difference is in the substances used to fill or pack them. You should discuss with your physician the use of generic drugs.

If you look at the bottom of the prescription sheet your doctor hands you to give to your pharmacist, you will notice a box with the letters "DAW" or "dispense as written." This means that the pharmacist should give the brand drug and not the generic. If you notice this is checked, ask your doctor if there is a generic drug available before you get to the pharmacy. The pharmacist can't legally give you the generic unless the doctor authorizes a new prescription.

So I can just switch to a generic version with no problems?

Not quite. Any drug that must maintain a level in your bloodstream (antiseizure meds, anticoagulants, certain cardiac meds, certain antipsychotic meds) must be maintained in the form you started. Switching from generic to brand name or vice versa could be fatal. The active components are the same, but your body may react differently with the nonactive ingredients and absorb not enough or too much of the active ingredient in the same dose.

Other types of drugs you should not switch from brand name to generic are:

- Coumadin (generic name: warfarin sodium)
- Synthroid (generic name: levothyroxine sodium)
- Lanoxin (generic name: digoxin), depending on the health of the patient

This is not because of any flaw in the generics. These drugs require a delicate balance in the system, so a change is not recommended if you can avoid it. If a doctor writes you a prescription for Synthroid, Coumadin, or Lanoxin, *get the generic the very first time,* or you may be stuck taking the overpriced brand name.

In any case, you should discuss with your physician the use of generic drugs before making a switch.

What if my medication has no generic equivalent?

Sometimes you may be stuck using the brand-name medication. However, there are some brand-name drugs without a generic that are in the same family of drugs that has a generic available, so ask your doctor if a similar drug (available in a generic version) could help you.

Additionally, sometimes a brand-name drug that doesn't have a generic is made of components that do have generics, and you can take those generics instead. For example, Ultracet contains acetaminophen along with the same drug as is found in Ultram (generic name: tramadol). It might save you money to get a prescription for tramadol and take over the counter (OTC) acetaminophen instead. If the doctor writes a prescription for acetaminophen, the pharmacist may be able to run the OTC acetaminophen through as a prescription so you don't have to pay sales tax on it (although you may have to pay a copayment, so check to be sure that this strategy really does save you money).

When does it make sense to use over-the-counter medications instead of prescription meds?

Many over-the-counter drugs once required a prescription. For example, the allergy medication Claritin can now be purchased without a prescription, although before its patent expired you needed a prescription. So, ask your doctor if there is an over-the-counter medication that you could use.

Also, be aware that sometimes the over-the-counter version of a medication is just a lower dose of a prescription drug. An example of this is adult ibuprofen, which comes in 200 mg strength while prescription strength is 400 to 800 mg a dose. It may be cheaper to simply take more of the over-the-counter medication (in order to match the prescription strength). Check with your doctor about this before trying it. Several stomach preparations, arthritis medications, and other drugs are now available over the counter in reduced strengths.

My grandmother cuts her pills in order to save on prescription costs. Does this strategy work?

Many prescription drugs actually cost the same (or very close) regardless of the dosage. So your 20 mg pill may cost the same as a 40 mg pill, and if you split the 40 mg pill in half, you would have two 20 mg pills, thus getting twice as many pills for the cost.

For example, both the 10 mg and 20 mg pills of lisinopril (Prinivil) for high blood pressure cost about $27 for a 30-day supply. If you need only 10 mg, you can buy the 20 mg versions and cut the pills in half, saving $15 per month.

But not all pills can be split without compromising their effectiveness. Some medications have a special coating, work on a time-release, or are in capsule form. Ask your doctor and pharmacist if you can split the pill. (But don't forget to actually split the pills before taking them!

You don't want to overdose yourself. Sometimes the pharmacy will split the pills for you, so ask.)

Done properly, pill cutting can save up to 50 percent of the cost of a medication. The following website can help calculate your savings: *www.excellusbcbs.com.*

I've heard of people traveling to Canada or Mexico to buy their medications for lower prices. Does this work?

For a variety of reasons, consumers often pay significantly less for medications purchased in Canada and Mexico. For example, Canada has laws capping how much drug manufacturers can charge for medications. Other factors, like trade laws and manufacturing costs, also play a role.

For years, Americans have been visiting foreign countries to buy prescription drugs that are too expensive or unavailable in the States. Americans are permitted to import a ninety-day supply of approved drugs from these countries for personal use. However, it is less clear whether you can import unapproved or experimental medications for personal use. Check with the Food and Drug Administration and your physician before making plans to import foreign drugs.

Keep in mind that drugs made and sold overseas may not adhere to the same manufacturing and storage standards as in the United States. Make sure you buy all of your prescription and nonprescription medications from a reputable pharmacy. Some pharmacies may relabel drugs, sell expired pills, or sell counterfeit pills. Be wary of scams, and don't buy something if it doesn't seem right.

Drugs that are subject to abuse (such as steroids, amphetamines, and some sedatives) are more tightly controlled. Always bring a copy of your doctor's prescription with you to smooth the way back.

Be aware that while you can bring medications back with you (as long as they are for personal use) you cannot have them sent to you (the U.S. government bans this practice).

The following websites can assist you in your importing process:

- *www.fda.gov/ForIndustry/ImportProgram/ucm173751.htm*
- *www.fda.gov/ora/import/pipinfo.htm*
- *www.cbp.gov/travel*

I've heard that some drug companies provide assistance for people who need their medications. How does that work?

Most major pharmaceutical companies participate in drug-assistance programs that will help low-income individuals pay for their medication. Each company has its own criteria, but if you can demonstrate true financial hardship, most companies will provide the drug at no charge (however, you must qualify for one of their programs, which generally requires an application process).

Partnership for Prescription Assistance (PPA) is a one-stop shop that helps people without insurance that covers prescriptions to get the medicines they need by providing information on a variety of public and private drug-assistance programs. As of now, forty-five pharmaceutical companies provide PPA with information for more than 150 programs. To find out more information about participating companies, you may go online to *www.pparx.org.*

Keep in mind that not all companies and programs may be represented in the PPA database. If your medication isn't on the PPA, you can call the manufacturer directly to find out what programs they may be offering that you may qualify for. Your doctor should be able to help you figure out the manufacturer.

You mentioned that prescriptions can cost different amounts at different pharmacies. How do I compare?

You can simply call various pharmacies and ask them to quote you a price on your medication. Not only do pharmacies differ in their charges, but some offer extra services such as a door-to-door delivery service for a small fee (or in some cases, for no extra charge). A no-frills pharmacy may be able to charge less than a full-service pharmacy, but no-frills doesn't always translate to lower cost. Check prices before making a decision.

Know the drug name, dosage, and quantity when you call. If you can't read the prescription or don't understand exactly what it means, have your doctor or a member of the office staff write it out for you.

It may make sense to purchase different drugs from different pharmacies, since there might be a vast difference in prices between medications; however, be very careful if you do this because you may add on additional hassles and potentially lose track of prescriptions.

It is always a good idea to carry around a list of the drugs you are taking, including over-the-counter medications and supplements such as minerals and vitamins. Be sure to show this list to the pharmacist before you submit your prescription so he or she can double check to be sure your medications do not interact with each other. If they do, the pharmacist can call your prescribing doctor and suggest a comparable medication that will not interact.

You may also want to check into stores such as Costco, Target, and Walmart for even lower prices on generic drugs than your local pharmacies. Although stores like Costco traditionally only open their discounts to members, some states require these stores to sell prescription medications to nonmembers. Many drugstore chains, including Kmart, Rite Aid, and Walmart, as well as some independent drugstores, will match the lowest price available in your area for prescription drugs. Kmart will even match prices from the Internet and mail-order pharmacies. That means it pays to comparison shop, then ask your favorite pharmacy if it will match the lowest price you find. Not all companies will match the best price you find. CVS stores wouldn't even match cheaper drug prices found on the company's own website.

Prescription drug prices can change, so keep in mind that the pharmacy that has the best price on a certain drug today may not have it tomorrow, or may be one of the most expensive places for other medications.

If you are a senior, ask your pharmacy if they offer a senior citizen discount or other discounts from organizations you may belong to (such as AARP). Consider all of these possibilities when comparing various pharmacies.

A helpful chart to help organize your findings while comparing prices with the methods found in this part can be located at *www .pharmacychecker.com.*

My medication doesn't have a generic version and even at the lowest-cost pharmacy, it's still expensive. Any other ideas for saving money on medications?

Remember that everything changes—prices fluctuate, patents expire, and so on. Once a year, bring all your drugs and nutritional supplements to your pharmacist and physician so they can suggest any less expensive alternatives. Sometimes inexpensive versions, including generics or older, well-established drugs, work as well as newer, higher-priced drugs. The doctor's review should focus first on whether you still need all your medications. It's not unusual for a person to start taking a drug such as an antianxiety medication for a specific symptom and to keep taking it even when it's no longer necessary.

Keep in mind that most good doctors will never try to push a medication on you and may not always remember your individual financial circumstance, since they see so many patients a day. Be sure to remind the doctor, especially when it comes to your medication, that you are trying to save some money and he or she will almost always try to help. Most doctors are unaware of the cost of the medications they prescribe. Unfortunately, the drug manufacturer representatives who frequent the doctor's offices often promote the newest, most expensive medications. These medications are not the only ones that could solve your medical problem, but unless you talk with your doctor, you may end up with an unnecessarily expensive medication. For example, if you've got allergies, you ask for a good allergy medication. The doctor prescribes Medication A, but Medication B, previously a prescription drug and now available over-the-counter and generic, may work just as well for your problem and is less than half the cost. Unknowingly, you have doubled the cost to you and/or your insurance company (which in turn translates into higher insurance premiums). So be aware, and always ask questions.

I see a lot of ads for Internet pharmacies. Are these a legitimate way to save money on prescription costs?

Internet pharmacies say they can offer savings because of the centralized warehousing for fulfilling orders and the efficiencies of scale. An example of this is Drugstore.com, which claims to save its customers 20 to 30 percent on most prescriptions.

The biggest bargains come from Canada, thanks to government price controls, which is why average discounts from the country can be as much as 67 percent cheaper than the normal U.S. prices. However (and this is a big however!) the Food and Drug Administration (FDA) bans the cross-border shipment of drugs into the United States. It sends warning letters to overseas pharmacies and alerts the Customs Service to watch out for packages from them.

While it is unlikely that you will be personally prosecuted (especially if you're ordering a nonnarcotic prescription), ordering medications from a pharmacy located in another country is not your best bet for saving money.

Also, it's possible that a drug manufactured in another country is not of the same quality as one produced in the United States and sold in your local pharmacy.

However, all of that doesn't mean you can't save money using an Internet pharmacy based in the States. You may be able to do so. The key is to comparison shop carefully.

I want to try using an Internet pharmacy. What should I know first?

It's a good idea to do your due diligence and select an Internet pharmacy that is reputable and reliable. Here are some tips:

- Only buy from sites that require prescriptions from a physician or other authorized healthcare provider. A good Internet pharmacy will contact your doctor's office to verify the prescription. A written verification policy is usually posted on the website. This process isn't as convenient as it could be, because most doctors aren't yet equipped for electronic transmission. So you still have to mail in the prescription or have your doctor call or fax the Internet pharmacy.

- Don't provide any personally identifiable information (social security number, credit card, medical history) unless you are confident that the site will protect it. Make sure the site does not share your information with others without your permission.

As for the confidentiality of the information being exchanged, Internet pharmacies employ similar security procedures as most other e-commerce sites. Drugstore.com, for instance, makes sure employee access to the data is on a need-to-know basis. The company also employs the current security industry's best practices, which include regular security audits.

- If the website looks amateur, chances are the company is, too. The website should provide valid information about drug interactions and should post an address or phone number you can call to reach a human being (such as a licensed pharmacist) who can answer your questions. Be sure to test this by calling this number or sending an e-mail to the company with a general question to see how they respond. Look for efficiency and accuracy.

- Make sure customer service policies are posted and that you understand them. For example, a good Internet pharmacy will let you know if a generic version of your medication becomes available.

- Buy only from U.S.-based sites. It's illegal and unsafe to buy prescription medicines from foreign sites. Look for where the company does business, and be sure that place exists. Using Google maps, you can find out if the address really exists.

- Does the website have a Verified Internet Pharmacy Practice Sites seal?

This seal is one of the best ways to find a safe online drugstore. The Verified Internet Pharmacy Practice Sites (VIPPS) seal demonstrates that a pharmacy has been certified by the National Association of Boards of Pharmacy (NABP), which represents the fifty state boards of pharmacy. To be included in the program, a pharmacy must agree to encourage patient-pharmacist communication and to provide safe storage and shipment for its drugs, among other things. The program also confirms the pharmacies' state licenses and inspects their facilities.

At the time of this book being written, there were only thirteen Internet pharmacies with the VIPPS seal, including Drugstore.com Inc. (*www.drugstore.com*) and Familymeds.com (*www.familymeds.com*).

To find out more information about the VIPPS seal and safe web pharmacies, visit *www.nabp.net/programs*.

- Don't use an Internet pharmacy that will prescribe drugs for you. While most states have no specific law against prescribing drugs online based on inadequate patient-physician interaction, a number of states, including Florida, are considering passing new laws barring the practice. Others, like North Carolina and California, interpret their present laws to prohibit such prescribing of drugs, ruling that it isn't a proper medical practice. On that basis, many state medical boards and pharmacy boards are cracking down on physicians and pharmacists who prescribe and dispense drugs using only an online questionnaire. The Florida State Pharmacy Board is considering passing a rule to discipline pharmacists who fill prescriptions that they know are written based solely on online physician-patient interactions.

For more information about buying drugs online, see the FDA's guide at: *www.fda.gov/oc/buyonline/default.htm.*

HOW TO CONTROL THE COST OF MEDICAL PROCEDURES

I need a medical procedure done on an outpatient basis, but I know that even a minor procedure can still cost thousands. How do I control my costs?

Talk to the prescribing doctor. Be sure you understand what is needed and all your options. For example, a doctor may not need to run certain tests and is only doing so to confirm a diagnosis. Is the procedure necessary, or do you think you need a second opinion? Never be afraid of upsetting your doctor if you get another opinion. A good, confident doctor will always encourage you to get that second opinion because he or she knows you will come back. In addition, if there is a new procedure being used, he or she will want to know about it, and become more educated in that area.

A website that can give you some guidance on what tests and procedures may be appropriate for certain conditions is *www.choosing wisely.org/doctor-patient-lists/*.

See Part 3 for more information on determining if you really need a certain test, procedure, or treatment.

Unfortunately, I do have to have the procedure done. What else can I do to control my costs?

Shop around. Ask your doctor where he or she has privileges and contact those facilities for a little comparison-shopping. You may be surprised to find that facilities have varying rates. If you find one that is lower than another, ask your doctor to perform the procedure there.

How do you do this comparison shopping? Call up the facilities and start documenting prices. Call when the facility is not as busy (for some the morning is best, for others, mid-morning is even better). If you don't have insurance, be sure to mention that you want the cash rate and be honest about your financial situation. You might be surprised at the difference between the insurance rate and the cash rate. Many times, a facility will charge more if you have insurance. Often you can get even more of a discount if you pay for the procedure in full up front. Some facilities will even lower their prices if you can accommodate their times, such as having the procedure done at a slow time, or at a less desirable time of day or even time of year.

Some doctors may also be familiar with the facility's rates, so be sure to let them know what you are doing, and they may be able to save you some legwork. Again, always double check with your insurance to be sure the insurance company covers the facility you want to go with.

I've found the most reasonably priced facility, but it's still going to be expensive! What else can I do?

Negotiate! You've done it with your car and your house, why not your medical bills? Keep in mind you may be calling a few different groups such as the facility, the surgeon, the radiologist, and the anesthesiologist. Let them know about your situation (that you are concerned about finances) and ask them what their best price is.

Be sure to tell your doctor if you do not have insurance. Just because you told his staff does not mean he or she knows. Most doctors will work with you to help minimize your bill, especially if you are paying cash at the time of the visit. If you are having a procedure done at a hospital, the doctor may be able to help you work something out with the hospital administration. If not, perhaps he can lessen his charges, and you might end up saving 20 to 40 percent. You should not have to pay more than an HMO or government-negotiated price for services rendered.

Your doctor can save you a great deal of financial headache if you are open and honest with him or her. Keep in mind that most doctors go into the medical field because they enjoy helping people, so if you ask, you may be pleasantly surprised how your doctor could help you, as well as be your biggest ally in time of need.

When trying to get the best price for a procedure, it can be hard to know what a procedure "should" cost. A good place to find out a reasonable price for a procedure is Healthcare Bluebook: *www.health carebluebook.com*. The Centers for Medicare and Medicaid Services have information on negotiated rates for Medicare and Medicaid at *www.cms.gov/apps/physician-fee-schedule/license-agreement.aspx*.

Once you've negotiated a fair price, get it in writing! Sometimes the healthcare provider forgets to communicate with his or her billing department, or may not even deal with billing. Be sure you get your agreement in writing from the person you negotiated with so you have proof when the billing department sends you a huge bill by accident. Take down names, dates, as well as summaries of all correspondences.

A great tool you can use when negotiating is the price estimate form: *www.healthcarebluebook.com*.

Even if I could get my doctor and the hospital to reduce their bills by 50 percent, I still couldn't afford the procedure I need. Now what?

Most hospitals have patient advocacy/charity care programs that can help you pay for your hospital bills. Be sure to ask before you have the procedure done, as you may have to make an application or provide documentation of your circumstances.

One type of program that provides federal funding to hospitals, nursing homes, and other facilities to offer free care is the Hill-Burton program. These facilities choose the specific services that they will offer for free or lower cost to those that qualify. To find out the closest Hill-Burton facility near you, visit *www.hrsa.gov/gethealthcare/index .html* or call 877-464-4772.

In addition, some public hospitals offer care specifically to those who are uninsured or have lower income. A list of these hospitals can be found at the National Association of Public Hospitals and Health Systems, *www.essentialhospitals.org/about-americas-essential-hospitals/listing -of-americas-essential-hospitals-members/.*

Call the patient services department or get in touch with the hospital's social worker and ask to be assisted in finding a financial program that may be available to you.

In addition to the hospital having charity care available, there are various types of state programs that assist individuals with financial difficulties to access proper medical care. In order to find out what programs exist and keep up with changes in your state, contact your state Department of Health or your local Medicaid office. A website that can help identify some state medical assistance programs as well as pharmaceutical companies cooperating with these programs is the directory to the Medical Research Assistant: *www.ec-online.net/ Assistants/medresassistant.htm.*

I don't have insurance but I can pay cash for my procedure. Is this the best way to go?

You can often save money if you pay cash up front and ask for a discount for doing so. Most doctors spend thousands each year on writing off unpaid bills, hiring bill collectors, and paying credit-card processing fees. Just hiring an attorney to file judgment against you for an unpaid bill can cost the doctor upward of 50 percent of the bill.

By paying cash up front, you're not only guaranteeing payment but eliminating the paperwork for the doctor. In most cases, you can negotiate up to a 50 percent discount on your bill.

Even if you haven't negotiated a discounted rate ahead of time, you may be able to reduce your costs. If you receive a bill for a procedure that cost $4,000, call your doctor and offer $2,000 in cash. Nine out of ten times he or she will accept as it is better to take the cash offer than to try to collect the money in other ways.

I'd like to be able to pay cash up front for the procedure, but I can't. What about a payment plan?

Yes, a payment plan can be a good alternative, and some doctors offer these. Be sure you agree to all the terms of the plan and that there are no hidden costs involved such as high interest rates. If you need a procedure done that costs $4,000, don't end up paying $8,000 in installments!

If you think you are going to miss a payment, call first and be honest about when you can pay. Most doctors would rather help you than send you to collections.

I'm tapped out. It would take me a hundred years to pay back this bill. What else can I do?

Start your own campaign. In the past few years, crowd funding has become more popular due to social media. This is done by starting a website or a profile with a story of how you got into your medical debt and how much you need to pay for your medical bills. There are people out there that may be touched by your situation and will help you out. Instead of giving donations to a larger organization, some people would rather have a more personal connection to the person they are helping.

Some companies that can help you start a crowd-funding campaign include You Caring (*www.youcaring.com/medical-fundraising*); Giving Forward (*www.giveforward.com/cause/raise-money-for-medical-expenses*); and Fundrazr (*fundrazr.com/pages/raise-money-for-healthcare*). Healfundr.com (*www.healfundr.org*) not only verifies the campaigner's diagnosis, but ensures that the funds raised go to pay legitimate medical expenses, and also keeps the administrative costs low. Unlike some other websites, the donors also control where the excess funds go, if there are any.

I'm going to need crutches (wheelchair/ other durable equipment) after my surgery. What's the least expensive way for me to get them?

In general, it's best to buy your own medical equipment. Hospitals charge a significant markup on equipment like crutches or braces, so you're almost always better off buying them on your own. Ask around your local area; charitable groups and medical clinics will often donate equipment to those in need. Don't forget to ask around at medical facilities, especially a physical therapy office that may be moving offices or updating equipment.

CONTROLLING MEDICAL COSTS WHEN YOU HAVE A CHRONIC DISEASE

I have a chronic medical condition that costs me a fair amount of money each year to treat. What's the best step I can take to help control those costs?

Look for local chronic disease groups. If you or a member of your family has a chronic disease, it can be financially as well as emotionally draining. Look for a local or even national support group that may provide guidance on how to lower treatment costs, find an inexpensive health insurance plan, or even deal with your medical bills. These groups can be found through your local state department; the Centers for Disease Control and Prevention at *www.cdc.gov/DiseasesConditions* (or call 800-232-4636); or the National Association of Chronic Disease Directors at *www.chronicdisease.org* (or call 770-458-7400).

Many times, advocacy organizations are difficult to find because they do not have the money to advertise and rely on members of their community to spread the word. Once you are diagnosed with a particular disease, be sure to do a little research on organizations or support groups that may be advocates in your community.

What else would you recommend I do to help control the costs associated with my chronic disease?

There are several things you can do to make dealing with the financial impact of a chronic disease easier to manage.

- Find an advocate, whether this is a doctor, family member, friend, or an organization. Find someone who can be your spokesperson and who understands your condition and wishes, and who can remain calm, no matter how passionate they are about getting the best care for you. If necessary, be sure this person has the right authorization (such as a power of attorney) to make healthcare decisions if you become incapacitated.

- Stay organized. The more organized you stay, the more you can save in time while lowering your stress level, especially when reviewing bills for potential mistakes.
- Keep up with your bills. You'll be able to spot any problems as soon as they arrive and can correct them.
- Keep communicating and stay calm. Use the "smile and dial" method. Pick up the phone and smile while you double check with your "friends in billing." People are human and make mistakes. Treat them kindly even if you're frustrated.
- Find the right team to help manage your illness, whether this means a specialist who knows your disease or local providers who can donate time and treatments for free or at a discount.

HOW TO CONTROL COSTS FOR MENTAL HEALTHCARE

In the past, my health insurance hasn't had much in the way of mental health benefits. How has that changed with the ACA?

Luckily, mental and behavioral health (including substance abuse) services are now considered one of the ten essential health benefits that health insurance plans in the Marketplace must carry. The specifics depend on the state you live in, but insurance plans in the Marketplace must follow these rules:

- They cannot deny you coverage or charge you more just because you have a preexisting condition.
- Coverage begins as soon as your Marketplace coverage is in effect.
- Plans can't apply yearly or lifetime dollar limits on coverage of essential health benefits, which includes benefits for mental health and substance use disorder services.
- Plans cannot apply financial (deductible, copayments, coinsurance, and out-of-pocket) treatment (number of days or visits covered) or care management (prior authorizations) limits to mental health and substance abuse services that are more restrictive than limits applied to medical and surgical services.

If you feel your plan is not being compliant under the new Affordable Care Act rules, you can file an appeal at *parityispersonal.org*; however, if you have health insurance through your employer, your appeal will most likely be handled by the Federal Labor Department.

More information about how to get mental health treatment can be found at *www.mentalhealth.gov*.

Unfortunately, my plan is grandfathered and I don't have the mental health benefits that the Marketplace plans have. How can I get help without going broke?

If you have a plan that is not through the Marketplace or you cannot find a therapist you like under your plan that accepts your insurance, contact your county mental health department, which coordinates mental healthcare and can help you find affordable treatment.

Keep in mind that most health plans limit mental-health therapist coverage to a certain amount of visits per year, and you may need more, which can be very costly. If you go to a certified counselor or a clinical social worker instead, you might be able to cut your bill in half. Most studies have found no difference in the effectiveness.

You may also be able to locate a free mental health clinic center on the Federal Substance Abuse and Mental Health Services Administration website at: *www.findtreatment.samhsa.gov/MHTreatment Locator/faces/quickSearch.jspx.*

In addition, Medicaid offers discounted mental health services such as psychotherapy, counseling, mental and behavioral health inpatient services, and substance use disorder treatments for those who qualify.

HOW TO CONTROL DENTAL COSTS

How can I save on routine dental care?

Find out what you may need in terms of x-rays and if you can get them at an imaging center nearby that may be cheaper. Then bring the films or have the digital files sent to your dentist. Know that when you shop around, the cost of those x-rays can range from $55 to $300 for each film. That's a big difference!

Many dentists require a full mouth series, which can be as many as twenty x-rays, but this may not be necessary every time you go in. Make sure the dentist gives you a good reason why it should be done each time and ask if it can be limited to once a year or perhaps even less.

In addition, you may be able to get a deal if you are considered a new patient. If you have a dentist you have been using for years, ask if you can use this new patient discount.

If you have cavities, request amalgam rather than resin fillers. Amalgam tends to be cheaper and in many cases lasts much longer, too.

Finally, just because your dentist has the latest and greatest technology, this is no reason you should have to pay a significantly higher price to get a similar result. Some older equipment is just as good as the new equipment out there. For example, traditional impression-taking and crown-fabricating techniques have resulted in restorations lasting more than forty years.

My dentist says I need to have an expensive procedure done. How can I get the procedure without breaking the bank?

Most people do not go to the dentist until something goes wrong in their mouth, and unfortunately, that is when it can become extremely costly. Read the section earlier in this part called "How to Control the Cost of Medical Procedures" to get some idea of how you can keep a lid on expenses.

I've heard about a clinical trial for a dental problem I'm having. Can I save money by doing this?

Yes, you can. Clinical trials may be a great way to get a newer procedure done at a fraction of the cost. Sometimes organizations such as the National Institutes of Dental and Craniofacial Research (NIDCR) seek volunteers with specific dental, oral, and craniofacial conditions to participate in clinical trials. If you qualify for a clinical trial, you can get limited free or low-cost dental treatment for the particular condition. To find out if there are any NIDCR clinical trials that you might fit into, visit *www.clinicaltrials.gov.*

Unfortunately, my insurance doesn't cover dental care and I don't have a lot of extra money to spend. What else can I do to find less-expensive dental care?

Dental schools can also be a good source of quality, reduced-cost dental treatment. A list of these teaching facilities, accredited by the American Dental Association (ADA), can be found at *www .ada.org/267.aspx.* These clinics allow dental students to gain experience treating patients at a reduced cost, while being supervised by a licensed dentist. In addition, dental hygiene schools provide similar programs. These can be found on the American Dental Hygienists' Association website: *www.adha.org/dental-hygiene-programs.*

Unfortunately, you might have to wait a while for the next available appointment, so call ahead of time and be sure to block out a few hours, because you might be spending a little extra time in the chair since these students are learning.

Health Resources and Services (*www.hrsa.gov* or 1-888-Ask-HRSA) supports federally funded community health centers across the country that provide free or reduced-cost health services, including dental care. You can find one nearby at this link: *www.findahealth center.hrsa.gov/Search_HCC.aspx*.

If you are enrolled in Medicare, Medicaid, or the Children's Health Insurance Program (CHIP), you may be eligible for certain types of dental care, including dental emergencies. For state-specific information, visit *www.medicaid.gov/Medicaid-CHIP-Program-Information/By -Topics/Benefits/Dental-Care.html*.

If you have children under the age of nineteen who are enrolled in the CHIP program, be sure to check to see what dental coverage your children might be eligible for at *www.medicaid.gov/Medicaid -CHIP-Program-Information/By-Topics/Childrens-Health-Insurance -Program-CHIP/CHIP-Benefits.html*. Benefits will vary from state to state.

Even if you are not enrolled in any of these government programs, check your state or local health department to see what new programs might have evolved in your area that provide free or low-cost dental services.

In addition, charitable organizations such as the United Way (*www.unitedway.org*) may be able to direct you to some programs that can provide assistance with dental care.

USING PREVENTION TO CONTROL HEALTHCARE COSTS

I often hear that preventative medicine is less costly than dealing with problems after they become problems. What are some ways I can use prevention to control my healthcare costs?

A great way to get started is by having a thorough exam done by your physician. Use this as an opportunity to ask a lot of questions and get started on a plan to improve or maintain your overall health.

Here are some of the questions you should be asking during your that checkup:

- Are all of your signs within the accepted limits, or at least what appears to be your normal? This would include some of the following:
  - Your body-mass index (BMI), which will tell you if your weight is appropriate for your height
  - Your blood pressure and your pulse, to see if your heart is beating regularly and if your blood pressure is lower or higher than normal (normal = 120/80 mm Hg); however, be sure your doctor considers your baseline, since a significant change in what is considered normal for you may indicate issues

- Your breathing can determine if your lungs are working efficiently, sounds shallow, labored, or rapid
- Your skin tone and nails, whose color, texture, and appearance give clues to underlying disorders of your vital organs
- Is your health better, the same, or worse since your last checkup?
- What are the best ways you can maintain your health or manage your condition if you have one? You should ask for advice on:
  - Your diet and exercise
  - Stress-management tips to ease chronic tension and anxiety that can potentially create a host of ills
- Given your personal and family medical history, do you have a higher than normal risk for certain illnesses? You should review with your doctor:
  - Your family medical history, including your grandparents, parents, or siblings who had heart attacks, strokes, diabetes, breast or prostate cancers, and other illnesses
  - Your personal medical history, which may include a childhood history of sunburn, tuberculosis, chicken pox, severe allergies, or high fevers that may be risk factors for diseases later in life. In addition, be sure to mention if you were hospitalized, had surgery, or have been tested positive for allergies to drugs or food.
- Ask about vaccines you might have had in the past or may need in the future.
- Be sure to mention if you have been out of the country or exposed to anyone from out of the country recently. This is something many patients forget to mention when they

come in sick, and can help the doctor pinpoint the route or cause of a sudden sickness.

- Given your age and health, what symptoms may indicate the onset of an illness mentally or physically?
- Given your medical status, what symptoms may indicate a medical emergency?
- What screenings should you have? Your doctor may recommend a mammogram for breast cancer, a bone density scan for osteoporosis, a colonoscopy or sigmoidoscopy for colorectal cancer, a blood test for prostate-specific antigens that may indicate prostate cancer, a Pap smear to look for irregular cervical cells, or blood tests for cholesterol and other markers for cardiovascular disease.
- Should you be seeing a specialist for any reason, such as an endocrinologist for potential thyroid or diabetic issues?
- What new therapies or changes in treatment such as medication should you investigate since your last checkup, and what are the costs?
- Should you get a flu shot? If you have one of a number of risk factors (such as age or a weak immune system), you may be strongly encouraged to get one.

Any other prevention suggestions?

Be proactive. If you have a family history of breast cancer, you may want to schedule your first mammogram at an earlier age than the recommended starting age of forty. By doing your first exam earlier, you can become more aware of what is normal and what is not, in terms of your body and baseline health. Thus, you will be more likely to notice a lump in your breast and to do something about it before it potentially becomes a more serious issue and costs you more money in treatments.

Some local healthcare facilities even have programs that provide uninsured women with free breast and cervical cancer screenings, even treatment if necessary. Also, the National Breast and Cervical Cancer Early Detection Program allows women with low household income to receive free or low-cost mammograms and Pap smears. For more information, visit *www.cancer.org/healthy/findcancerearly/womens health/earlydetectionofspecificcancers/nbccedp.*

In addition, if you are prone to degenerative joint disease or even osteoporosis, you may want to invest in calcium supplements at an earlier age and be sure you are practicing the proper ways to work out ahead of time. A trip to the physical therapist can help with this, especially if you are already starting to feel back or arm pain.

If you are suffering from back pain and have a history of back issues, check with your insurance company about whether they'll cover a few sessions with a physical therapist. You may find that your insurance covers a certain amount of sessions. You can learn how to protect your back, how to properly work out, and other skills that will help you keep your back healthy.

These are just some basic ideas to get you started. Think about medical problems that run in your family, or that you've experienced previously, and what you can do to help ensure that you stay healthy. Keep in mind that many medical problems can be prevented, or at least helped, through a good diet and exercise program.

Since my father ended up with skin cancer, I know that one of the best preventions for that is sunscreen. But how do I know which is best?

Here are some tips for purchasing and using sunscreen:

- Get the date. Sunscreen loses its effectiveness over time, so be sure it's within its expiration date before you use it. If you can't find a date, look for signs of deterioration such as a change in color or consistency. If your sunscreen has been exposed to extreme temperatures, it is probably better to get rid of it. A good rule is to buy new sunscreen every year. And don't forget to use it year-round, not just in the summer!
- Use broad-spectrum sunscreen. Many people think that they just need to get a sunscreen with a high "sun protection factor" (SPF), but that only measures the ability of a sunscreen to block UVB rays. Those rays cause sunburns, but UVA rays are the ones linked to skin damage (and thus potentially to cancer). So, pick a sunscreen that blocks both UVA and UVB rays.
- Check the active ingredients. Only two forms of active ingredients are approved by the Food and Drug Administration (FDA) in most sunscreens: mineral and chemical filters. Even though chemical filters (such as avobenzone, oxybenzone, and octinoxate) are more common, it is the mineral filters, such as zinc oxide and titanium dioxide, that have been deemed the safer option. Unlike most chemical filters, these mineral filters cover both UVA and UVB rays.

- Chose a sunscreen that includes Vitamin E. Not only does Vitamin E work as a moisturizer for your skin, but it has been proven to help absorb cancer-causing free radicals that may occur from sun exposure. Consider this a bonus when purchasing your sunscreen.
- Pick a sunscreen without parabens, a type of preservative that can be toxic. Try to find a sunscreen that uses essential oils as preservatives.
- Use enough. Make sure you use enough sunscreen to completely cover your skin, including your skin under your T-shirt, since the sun's damaging rays can penetrate your clothing. Remember to apply it at least thirty minutes before going out into the sun. You should also reapply your sunscreen every ninety minutes or so, more often if you sweat a lot or take a dip in the pool.

Can taking an aspirin a day really prevent a heart attack?

Yes, that cheap little pill may save you $25,000 later—that's the average cost of treating a heart attack. One baby aspirin (81 mg) a day keeps the cardiologist at bay. You have probably heard that if you are a man over the age of forty or a woman past menopause, a smoker, have high blood pressure, or a family history of heart disease, you can lower your risk of a heart attack by taking an aspirin every day or every other day. That is true.

In addition, your doctor may recommend an aspirin a day if you've already had a heart attack or stroke, have been treated for coronary artery disease (with a stent or bypass), are at risk for having a heart attack, or are an older adult with diabetes.

Be aware that *stopping* your aspirin-a-day ritual can increase your risk of heart attack, particularly if you've had heart trouble. Talk to your doctor before making any changes, because stopping suddenly can trigger a blood clot.

If you do embark on an aspirin-a-day plan, but can't use aspirin for whatever reason, try a nonsteroidal anti-inflammatory medication (NSAID), such as ibuprofen (Motrin, Advil) and naproxen (Aleve). Keep in mind that regular use of NSAID medications can increase your bleeding risk, as can other medications you may take for aches and pains (such as ibuprofen or Tylenol).

It's best not to combine ibuprofen with aspirin. Either take it eight hours before or thirty minutes after the aspirin.

It may be beneficial for you to keep an aspirin handy at all times if you have coronary artery disease (CAD). In the case of a heart attack/chest pain (be sure your doctor helps you distinguish this from heartburn) or stroke, one adult-strength (325 mg) aspirin—preferably in a chewable form since it is absorbed in the blood stream faster—may buy you some extra time when calling 911 by helping prevent the formation of blood clots. Seconds mean everything when someone is suffering from a heart attack or stroke!

Consult with your doctor before you begin using aspirin as preventative medicine, because it may not be advisable if you have a bleeding or clotting disorder, bleeding stomach ulcers, or other problems. In addition, let your doctor know your drinking habits and all dietary supplements you are taking, as well as other medications you are on, because some combinations can be deadly.

Anything else?

It's the little things that make a difference in the quality of your life. Here are just a few ideas that can help you save money and stay healthy.

- Drink from the tap and eat real food. Americans spend billions of dollars a year on bottled water, sports bars, and nutritional supplements. Unfortunately, most of that stuff has very little proven benefit. So ditch the sports drinks, drink from the tap, and tote around fresh fruits and vegetables.
- Wash your hands. Americans pay huge amounts of money for cold and flu remedies but routinely neglect the best preventative treatment of all: soap and water. Get into the habit of scrubbing your hands for about twenty seconds, especially around the nails, before eating or handling food and after contact with any potential contaminants.
- Let your boss help. Take advantage of any wellness benefits that your employer or your insurance company offers, including smoking cessation classes, discounts on gym memberships, health risk assessments, and annual flu shots.
- Adult-proof your home. Home accidents rank among the top reasons for visits to the emergency room. Here are some easy ways to make your home safer and avoid a trip to the ER:
  - Install handrails along both sides of the stairs
  - Use nightlights
  - Put nonslip strips on tubs
  - Check smoke alarm batteries every month
  - Keep candles at least three feet from anything that can burn
  - Visit the home page of the National Safety Council (*www.nsc.org/safety_home*) for more tips.

- Brush and floss daily. It's the best way to prevent periodontal disease and keep your teeth white. Be sure to replace your toothbrush every few weeks!
- Follow doctor's orders. According to the *Merck Manual of Medical Information*, more than half of all patients don't follow instructions about taking medicine, which results in about 10 percent of hospital visits a year. These incidents could be avoided by listening to your doctor and following instructions. If you find you do not like your doctor, or worse, do not trust your doctor, start searching for a new one immediately.

CONCLUSION

I hope you found the information in this book useful and that your questions about the Affordable Care Act have been answered. While it may seem complicated and confusing at first, understanding the ACA means you can get the most out of it—the best medical care for the most affordable price. Recognizing how the law affects you has a big payoff, so it's worth taking the time to learn what it means on a personal level.

In this book, I described the ACA—what it does and what it means for individuals. I showed you everything you need to know to select a healthcare plan, described the ways you can get the best care possible from your team of healthcare providers, and gave you as much information as I could about how to control your healthcare costs.

By now, you've probably taken to heart something I said over and over in many different ways: The most important thing you can do for your health is to take action! Remember, you're in charge. If you don't like your plan, you can change it. If you stop trusting your doctor, you can find a new one. If you're not sure how you can afford a treatment, you can choose one of a wide variety of options to help you solve that problem.

You have a lot of possibilities for dealing with healthcare issues. Now's the time to start making some of those decisions!

RESOURCES

Following is a list of resources to help you find out more information about everything covered in this book.

THE AFFORDABLE CARE ACT

- You can find out what kind of state exchange/marketplace you are living in by going to *www.statereforum.org*.
- Each state decides the specifics of coverage of essential health benefits. You can check the guidelines for your state at *www.cms.gov/CCIIO/Resources/Data-Resources/ehb.html*.
- Mental health and substance use disorder services, including behavioral health treatment, are covered under the ACA. For more information, go to *www.mentalhealth.gov*.
- Preventive and wellness services and chronic disease management are covered under the ACA. For more detail on this, go to *www.healthcare.gov/what-are-my-preventive-care -benefits/*.
- You'll be charged a penalty for not having insurance unless you qualify for an exemption. For more information and to find the forms you need to apply for an exemption, go to *www.healthcare.gov/exemptions/*.
- One exemption is if your income is below the income tax return filing requirement. Here is a tool to help determine if you are required to file a federal tax return: *www.irs.gov/ uac/Do-I-Need-to-File-a-Tax-Return%3F*.
- More on hardship exemptions can be found here: *www.irs .gov/uac/Individual-Shared-Responsibility-Provision*.

- More information about not having health insurance can be found at *www.healthcare.gov/what-if-someone-doesnt-have-health-coverage-in-2014/*. In addition, you can use the handy "penalty calculator" found here: *www.calculator.taxpolicy center.org/*.
- Whether you are eligible for subsidies depends partly on your adjusted gross income. For more information on how to calculate your modified AGI, the IRS website provides this article: *www.irs.com/articles/what-modified-adjusted-gross -income*.
- You can shop for plans on *www.healthcare.gov*. Depending on which plan you select and what information you put in, the site will tell you whether or not you qualify for subsidies.
- If you are lower income, you may qualify for Medicaid. To find out if your state is expanding Medicaid coverage, go to *www.healthcare.gov/what-if-my-state-is-not-expanding -medicaid/*.
- If you don't qualify for Medicaid, you may be able to get low-cost healthcare at a Community Health Center near you. Here's the link to click to find out more about this: *www .healthcare.gov/where-can-i-get-free-or-low-cost-care/*. Here is a helpful subsidy calculator to see if you qualify: *www.kff.org/ interactive/subsidy-calculator/*.
- To apply for coverage through the insurance exchange, go to *www.healthcare.gov/how-do-i-apply-for-marketplace-coverage/*.
- You may qualify for a tax credit for purchasing health insurance through the Marketplace. For more information, go to *www.irs.gov/uac/The-Premium-Tax-Credit*.
- For a summary of ACA costs state by state, go to *www.legal consumer.com/obamacare/welcome.php*.
- If you purchased an individual health insurance policy on or before March 23, 2010, you may be able to keep it.

These plans are "grandfathered" into the system set up by the ACA. For more on grandfathered plans, look at *www .healthcare.gov/what-if-i-have-a-grandfathered-health-plan/*.

- Grandfathered plans may not include the essential coverage mandated by the ACA. For more information, go to *www.healthcare.gov/how-does-the-health-care-law-protect-me /#part=8*.

- Grandfathered plans that you purchase as an individual policy can deny you coverage or increase your premiums for preexisting conditions you may have. For more information, go to *www.healthcare.gov/how-does-the-health-care-law-protect -me/#part=3*.

- Grandfathered plans aren't obligated to let the provider join. For more information, go to *www.healthcare.gov/how -does-the-health-care-law-protect-me/#part=6*.

- Grandfathered plans can set annual or lifetime coverage expense limits for essential health benefits. For more information, go to *www.healthcare.gov/how-does-the-health-care -law-protect-me/#part=9*.

- For more information on appealing Marketplace decisions (for example, whether you're eligible to enroll outside the open enrollment period), go to *www.healthcare.gov/can-i -appeal-a-marketplace-decision/*.

- If you want to appeal a decision made by your health insurance plan, visit *www.hhs.gov/healthcare/rights/appeal/ appealing-health-plan-decisions.html* or call 1-800-318-2596 (or TTY: 1-855-889-4325). You can file a request electronically through *www.externalappeal.com*. If you need more help filling out your external review, your state's Consumer Assistance Program (CAP) or department of insurance may be able to help you.

- Under the Affordable Care Act, every state must provide comprehensive coverage for children. Go to your state to find out more details on your specific program: *www.insure kidsnow.gov/state/index.html.*

- Companies that have employees in more than one state, or individuals who are planning to move, may want to find an insurance plan that is offered in multiple states. For more information, go to *www.opm/gov/healthcare-insurance/multi -state-plan-program.*

- Small business owners who offer health insurance may be eligible for tax credits. You can investigate this more by going to *www.healthcare.gov/what-is-the-shop-marketplace/* or call 1-800-706-7893, Monday through Friday, 9 A.M. to 5 P.M. EST. Use the Small Business Healthcare Credit Estimator at *www.taxpayeradvocate.irs.gov/calculator/SBHCTC.htm* to help you find out whether you're eligible for the credit and how much you might receive.

- For certain small business, if you choose not to offer a health plan, you must give your employees the form you'll find at *www.dol.gov/ebsa.* On the page, search for the PDF titled "FLSA Without Plans." If you offer your workers a health plan, distribute the form you can find on that site by searching for "FLSA With Plans."

- Small business owners are required to report the cost of health coverage under a group insurance plan on the employee's W-2 form. For more information on reporting, go to *www.irs.gov/uac/Form-W-2-Reporting-of-Employer -Sponsored-Health-Coverage.*

HOW TO SELECT THE RIGHT HEALTHCARE PLAN

- Your local state Insurance Department can help provide you with a list of HMOs in your area, as well as general background information on which healthcare services are covered. Visit *www.naic.org/state_web_map.htm*.
- For people using Health Savings Accounts, you can find out more about qualified medical expenses at *www.irs.gov*.
- There are limits to how much you can contribute to an HSA each year and other rules you must follow about setting up an HSA. More information about that can be found here: *www.irs.gov/publications/p969/ar02.html*.
- If you die, your spouse can use the money in your HSA to pay for his/her qualifying medical expenses. Be aware that different states have additional rules about the use of HSAs. You can find out more about that here: *www.healthinsurancefinders .com/cr_state_department_of_insurance.html*.
- You can find out more about the requirements and limits of a Flexible Spending Account at *www.irs.gov*; search for Publication 969.
- For more information on Medicaid services, and to find out if you qualify, visit *www.medicaid.gov*.
- Other state programs can be found through research. A good place to start is your state's Department of Health (*www.medicaid.gov/Medicaid-CHIP-Program-Information/By -State/By-State.html*).

- For specific information on the State Children's Health Insurance Program (SCHIP, usually called CHIP), go to *www.insurekidsnow.gov.*
- To find out if you're eligible for Medicare and how much premiums will cost, call 1-800-Medicare or 1-800-633-4227, or go to *www.medicare.gov/eligibilitypremiumcalc/.*
- To find out if you qualify for Social Security Disability Insurance (SSDI), go to *www.ssa/gov/pubs/10029.pdf.* To receive SSDI benefits, you'll have to get an official determination from the Social Security Administration. You can find the closest Social Security Office near you by going to *www.secure.ssa.gov/ICON/main.jsp.* You can complete an online application at *www.ssa.gov/pgm/disability.htm.*
- Figuring out if you're eligible for disability compensation from the government and if so, how much, can be complicated. One resource that can help is The National Organization of Social Security Claimants' Representatives (NOSSCR), *www.nosscr.org.*
- The National Disability Rights Network (*www.ndrn.org*) may be able to help you understand which disability programs are available in your state.
- To find out how much a health insurance plan through the Marketplace will cost, go to *www.healthcare.gov* and check out the available options. A quick way to get a reasonable guess as to what your premiums will be (in general, not tied to a specific plan) is to use the calculator at *www.laborcenter.berkeley.edu/healthpolicy/calculator/.*
- To find out more about your state's rules and regulations about insurance, go to *www.naic.org* and find the "States and Jurisdiction Map" tab at the top of the page. Then click on your state on the map of the United States. This will lead you to the website of your state's insurance commissioner,

where you can find out a lot about what's happening related to insurance.

- There are several websites that grade insurance companies in your area. The National Committee for Quality Assurance, whose focus is to "measure the quality of America's Health Care," offers an array of information on health insurance policies in your area at *www.reportcard.ncqa.org/plan/external/plansearch.aspx*. Consumer Reports also rates insurance companies at *http://consumerreports/org/cro/health/health-insurance/index.htm*.
- If you are unsure of the rules behind the free-look period in your state, visit *www.naic.org/state_web_map.htm* to find out if you can take advantage of the free-look period *before* fully committing to a health insurance plan.
- To find out when the next open enrollment period is, visit *www.healthcare.gov* and search "open enrollment."
- The National Association of Health Underwriters (*www.nahu.org*) or your local state commissioner may be able to put you in touch with a reputable health insurance broker in your area.

USING YOUR HEALTH INSURANCE BENEFITS WISELY

- A great resource for finding a doctor is *www.vitals.com*.
- The state medical boards or state medical licensure is usually located under the Department of Health in your state. They should have updated records of every doctor

practicing legally, as well as those practicing on a pending license. Two websites that contain contact information for all the state medical boards are *www.fsmb.org/state-medical-boards/contacts* and *www.docboard.org*.

- You can find out if your doctor is board-certified, which means he or she has completed a training program in a specialty and has passed some rigorous exams by checking online at *www.abms.org*. Or call the ABMS at 1-866-275-2267. You can also check on your doctor's certification by going to *www.certifacts.org*.

- Accreditation by the Joint Commission means that a healthcare organization (such as a hospital) has achieved a specific standard of patient care. Details about what that means can be found here: *www.qualitycheck.org/consumer/searchQCR.aspx*.

- If you feel the Joint Commission standards for care are not being met at a certain facility, you can contact the Joint Commission at *www.jointcommission.org/report_a_complaint.aspx*. For more information on the process, you can call 1-800-994-6610, fax 630.792.5636, or send an e-mail to *complaint@jointcommission.org*.

- To find out more about your specific health condition(s), you may want to tap into resources such as the National Institute of Health at *www.nih.gov* or to use information from a well respected institution like the Mayo Clinic (*www.mayoclinic.org*).

- For help making medical decisions, the Foundation for Informed Medical Decision Making (FIMDM) (*www.fimdm.org*) has developed shared decision-making programs for common medical problems (such as breast cancer and hormone replacement therapy) that enable you to make up your own mind while sharing all the pros and cons of various treatments.

- An online library that can answer a lot of your medical questions can be found at *www.healthlibrary.com*. Also, explore *www.webmd.com*.
- There are many useful websites that provide consumer health information. For example, at *www.healthfinder.gov* you'll find health topics from A to Z, a directory of services, and other useful links.
- To find a physician offering concierge healthcare, visit the American Academy of Private Physicians, *www.private physicians.com/#*. MDVIP is a network of concierge physicians. Find out more about them at *www.mdvip.com*.

CONTROLLING YOUR HEALTHCARE COSTS

- The IRS allows you to deduct medical bills that exceed 10 percent of your gross income. For more information, visit *www.irs.gov/taxtopics/tc502.html*.
- You can often save money by purchasing the generic version of a medication. A website that provides some guidance on generic drugs and their brand name equivalent is *www .disabled-world.com*.
- Done properly, pill cutting can save up to 50 percent of the cost of a medication. The following website can help calculate your savings: *www.excellusbcbs.com/*.
- Some Americans purchase medications in Canada or Mexico to save on costs. The following websites can assist

you in this process: *www.fda.gov/ForIndustry/ImportProgram /ucm173751.htm* and *www.cbp.gov/travel*.

- To find out more about companies participating in drug-assistance programs, go to *www.pparx.org/en/prescription_ assistance_programs* or call 1-888-477-2669.

- If you're comparison shopping for medication prices, a helpful chart to organize your findings can be located at *www.ec -online.net/knowledge/articles/drugchart.pdf*.

- At the time of this book being written, there were only thirteen Internet pharmacies with the VIPPS seal, including Drugstore.com Inc. (*www.drugstore.com*) and Familymeds .com (*www.familymeds.com*). To find out more information about the VIPPS seal and safe web pharmacies, visit *www .nabp.net/programs/accreditation/vipps*.

- For more information about buying drugs online, see the FDA's guide at *www.fda.gov/oc/buyonline/default.htm*.

- When negotiating a price for a procedure, a good place to start your comparison shopping is the Healthcare Bluebook: *www.healthcarebluebook.com*. The Centers for Medicare and Medicaid Services have information on negotiated rates for Medicare and Medicaid at *http://www.cms.gov/Understand the Reimbursement Process*.

- A great tool you can use when negotiating is this price estimate form: *www.healthcarebluebook.com/page_Pricing Agreement*.

- For lower cost medical care, you can find out the closest Hill-Burton facility near you by visiting *www.hrsa.gov/get healthcare/index.html* or calling 877-464-4772.

- Some public hospitals cater specifically to those who are uninsured or have lower income. A list of these hospitals can be found at the National Association of Public Hospitals and Health Systems, *www.essentialhospitals.org*.

- A website that can help identify some state medical assistance programs as well as pharmaceutical companies cooperating with these programs is the directory to the Medical Research Assistant: *www.ec-online.net/Assistants/medresassistant.htm*.

- Some companies that can help you start a crowd-funding campaign include You Caring (*www.youcaring.com/medical -fundraising*); Giving Forward (*www.giveforward.com/cause/raise-money-for-medical-expenses*); and Fundrazr (*www.fundrazr.com/pages/raise-money-for-healthcare*). Healfundr.org not only verifies the campaigner's diagnosis, but ensures that the funds raised go to pay legitimate medical expenses, and also keeps the administrative costs low.

- Support groups for chronic conditions can be found through your local state department; the Centers for Disease Control and Prevention at *www.cdc.gov/DiseasesConditions* (or call 800-232-4636); or the National Association of Chronic Disease Directors at *www.chronicdisease.org* (or call 770-458-7400).

- More information about how to get mental health treatment can be found at *www.mentalhealth.gov*.

- You may be able to locate a free mental health clinic center on The Federal Substance Abuse and Mental Health Services Administration website at *www.findtreatment.samhsa.gov*.

- To find out if there are any National Institutes of Dental and Craniofacial Research (NIDCR) clinical trials that you might fit into, visit *www.clinicaltrials.gov*.

- Dental schools can also be a good source of quality, reduced-cost dental treatment. A list of these teaching facilities, accredited by the American Dental Association (ADA), can be found at *www.ada.org/267.aspx*. Dental hygiene schools provide similar programs. These can be found on the American Dental Hygienists' Association website: *www.adha.org/dental-hygiene-programs*.

- Health Resources and Services (*www.hrsa.gov* or 1-888-Ask-HRSA) supports federally funded community health centers across the country that provide free or reduced-cost health services, including dental care. You can find one nearby at this link: *www.findahealthcenter.hrsa.gov*.
- If you are enrolled in Medicare, Medicaid, or the Children's Health Insurance Program (CHIP), you may be eligible for certain types of dental care, including dental emergencies. For state-specific information, visit *www.medicaid.gov /Medicaid-CHIP-Program-Information/By-Topics/Benefits/ Dental-Care.html*.
- If you have children under the age of nineteen who are enrolled in the CHIP program, be sure to check to see what dental coverage your children might be eligible for at *www .medicaid.gov/Medicaid-CHIP-Program-Information/By-Topics /Childrens-Health-Insurance-Program-CHIP/CHIP-Benefits .html*. Benefits will vary from state to state.
- Charitable organizations such as the United Way (*www .unitedway.org*) may be able to direct you to some programs that can provide assistance with dental (or other health) care.
- The National Breast and Cervical Cancer Early Detection Program allows women with low household income to receive free or low-cost mammograms and Pap smears. For more information, visit *www.cancer.org/healthy/findcancerearly /womenshealth/earlydetectionofspecificcancers/nbccedp*.
- Visit *www.homesafetycouncil.org* for tips on preventing accidents in the home.

APPENDIX
QUESTIONS TO A

SK YOUR POTENTIAL DOCTOR

Here is a brief checklist of questions you might want to ask the manager or other staff at the doctor's office, in addition to other questions you may have. Some of these items may be better answered by your health plan than by the doctor's office.

1. Which hospitals does the doctor use?
2. What are the office hours?
3. When is the doctor available?
4. When can I speak to office staff?
5. Does the doctor or someone else in the office speak the language that I am most comfortable speaking?
6. Who covers for the doctor when he or she is not available?
7. How long does it usually take to get a routine appointment?
8. How long might I need to wait in the office before seeing the doctor?
9. What happens if I need to cancel an appointment? Will I have to pay for it anyway?
10. Does the office send reminders about prevention tests? (For example: Pap smears.)
11. What do I do if I need urgent care or have an emergency?
12. Does the doctor (or a nurse or physician's assistant) give advice over the phone for common medical problems?

INDEX

ABOUT THE AUTHOR

Michelle Katz, MSN, LPN, is perhaps the most well-known healthcare advocate today. For more than fifteen years, Michelle has used her skills to make healthcare accessible, affordable, and understandable to thousands of Americans. She is well known for her work helping families across the country get out of medical debt. As a regular contributor to the *Real Money* segments on *ABC World News Tonight with Diane Sawyer,* her advice reaches millions.

Michelle is the author of two previous books on healthcare. In addition to her work on ABC, Michelle has appeared on the *CBS Evening News,* the *Today* show, *The Doctors, The Tavis Smiley Show,* and numerous local talk shows around the country. She is a regular contributor to the popular podcast *Informed Not Inflamed.*

A native of East Brunswick, New Jersey, Michelle is a graduate of George Mason University. She received her MSN from Georgetown University. She now resides in Los Angeles. Like her on Facebook and follow her on Twitter (@michellekatzmsn).